Emotional Fitness

A Counselor's Perspective

Betty Hamblen

ISBN: 978-1-4624-0363-9 (e)
ISBN: 978-1-4624-0364-6 (sc)

Library of Congress Control Number: 2012918916

Inspiring Voices books may be ordered through booksellers or by contacting:

Inspiring Voices
1663 Liberty Drive
Bloomington, IN 47403
www.inspiringvoices.com
1-(866) 697-5313

Printed in the United States of America

Inspiring Voices rev. date: 02/04/2013

To the memory of the late Roy and Lola Caver. Their humble example of service to others and of resolute loyalty to God continue to provide a steadying influence in the lives of their three children. I count it an undeserved blessing and a distinct privilege to be the middle one of those three.

Contents

Acknowledgments

My basis of knowledge about counseling has come from numerous researchers, writers, and teachers who labor to improve the lives of others through counseling and education. I owe those professionals a debt that is being repaid daily in my work as a counselor.

This manuscript would not be in any usable form without the earnest work of two close friends, Cory Collins and Dr. Bill Bagents. Both of them are diligent proof-readers. My gratitude for their friendship and their efforts on this book is boundless. I also owe many thanks to Monica Ross, my daughter and colleague, for her excellent and intense efforts in the final proofing. Her eagle eye in noticing small details that needed correction makes this book much more polished than my writing efforts deserve.

To my counseling colleagues at the Alpha Center, Rosemary, Bill, and Monica, I am deeply grateful. Their daily examples and advice help me to be a better counselor. They serve their clients with kindness and compassion. I thank them for their love for others, for numerous personal sacrifices, and for patience with their clients' needs and with my own shortcomings.

This book is in written form only because of the "push" from my family. My husband, Willie, has encouraged me through the years to put my ideas onto paper, gave suggestions, and even researched and contacted publishers. To my daughter, Ginger, I owe thanks for the title of this book and for her professional design of the cover. My children and grandchildren are a continual source of encouragement, support, and joy. They have taught me much about patience, about laughter, about the enduring joy of family. I love them all intensely.

Finally, I am deeply grateful to my clients. I have learned from them what profound courage it takes to search for a path out of confusion, to make healthier choices, to stitch together broken hearts, and to endure unbelievable pain. As we have talked, cried, and laughed together, we have forged special bonds. I feel honored and privileged that they allow me to share some of the most intense moments in their lives.

Notes

For counselors confidentiality is a supreme principle in the relationships they develop with clients. Therefore, names of clients used throughout this book are fictional and do not represent any living person. All counseling situations described are a composite of issues presented throughout the years of this author's counseling experience and are not intended to represent any person's individual circumstances.

Scripture quotations are from The Holy Bible, English Standard Version® (ESV®), copyright © 2001 by Crossway, a publishing ministry of Good News Publishers. Used by permission. All rights reserved.

Emotions and Fitness

Introduction

> *The noisy clash of voices sped from the reception area of our counseling center down the hallway and around the corner where I was completing paperwork before my next session with a new couple. If I could hear the noise from that distance and behind a closed door, I knew the argument was loud and intense.*
>
> *The office manager tapped softly and peeked around the door, her eyes wide and questioning. "Your clients are here," she whispered.*
>
> *I turned quickly to look at her. "You mean that is coming from my clients?!" She nodded and backed out the door, closing it quietly behind her.*
>
> *Whispering a brief prayer for peace for the couple and guidance for me, I went to meet my newest clients. Michelle sat in a chair to the left of the room, her face splotchy with tears and flushed with anger. Her foot bounced rapidly on the floor, as she chewed on her lower lip. Seth sat on the opposite side facing her, clenching and unclenching his jaw and fists. Neither one was looking at the other. Although their argument had ceased, I sensed this would be a challenging session. That sense proved to be accurate.*

This type of emotional scene plays out daily in counseling centers around the world, but it also occurs in living rooms, bedrooms, back yards, schools, grocery stores and business offices. Intense emotions are experienced not only by couples but by parents and children, by grandparents and grandchildren, by aunts and uncles, by employers and their workers, and by individuals with private issues that others may not recognize.

We counselors help guide clients toward finding resolutions to their problems, but a major part of our work involves helping clients learn to manage their intense or out-of-control emotions. This was true with Michelle and Seth. Until they dealt with their intense emotions, they would not be able to see beyond those emotions to focus on their actual problems. At the moment, their out-of-control emotions were their problem.

As we worked together through the next few sessions, I learned that Michelle and Seth were diligent about their physical health. They prepared nutritious meals at home, they exercised rigorously on a regular basis, and they were consistent about scheduling check-ups with their doctors and taking care of illnesses as they occurred. Being physically fit was important to them.

Their level of emotional fitness, however, was questionable. They, like many others, were neglecting an important aspect of their overall health. Both acknowledged that they had many issues and had difficulty talking about them. Michelle noted that they seemed hesitant to express their "real" feelings to each other.

While they had difficulty expressing issues of the heart, Seth indicated that both of them had no problem expressing intense emotions. Those emotions, he said, often had them on an "emotional roller coaster" for days and kept them apart. Seth and Michelle are no different from many clients that I regularly see who need a checkup for their emotional health.

Some of these clients experience intense emotions but may express them in inappropriate ways. Other clients appear lost in life, drifting along without purpose. Still others seem to be in an emotional low because they are adamantly pursuing goals that are not appropriate or beneficial for them in some way. Many of their behaviors are keeping them from being emotionally healthy most of the time.

The Relationship of Behaviors and Health

Most of us understand the link between behaviors and physical health. To be physically healthy, a person must eat food that is nourishing and suitable, maintain a reasonable weight, and be physically active, with a consistent routine of rest and sleep. A person who incorporates those behaviors into his life is generally healthy, barring any debilitating illness.

When everyday illnesses come, such a person seems able to bounce back to a normal state of health more quickly. Even when serious illnesses come, the one who is diligent about physical fitness can often recover more readily. That person's level of energy and stamina seems to remain higher than that of one who is not physically fit.

We can readily see that physical fitness requires certain behaviors on our part: eating well, exercising regularly, keeping our weight at a reasonable level and getting sufficient rest. *And* (this is the important part for long term health) we must be *consistent* in doing so. We must perform those actions regularly to get the most health benefits from them.

Emotional health is much like physical health. The premise of this book is that emotional fitness also requires certain behaviors practiced on a consistent basis. If those behaviors are practiced regularly, a person can more easily "bounce back" from emotional upsets, even serious ones. He can enjoy more emotional energy and stamina, and he can maintain healthier relationships.

Emotional health may even help to maintain physical health. In a story in a popular Sunday magazine, Dr. Henry S. Lodge noted that emotional health can impact physical health, particularly as it relates to aging.[1] Dr. Lodge, a faculty member at Columbia Medical School, has discovered an interesting link between emotions and the aging of the body. Part of Dr. Lodge's research has focused on factors that influence the growth and the decay of human cells. That research has resulted in two interesting findings.

Two Master Signals

According to Dr. Lodge, our cells have two master signals that tell them to grow. One of those signals is physical movement or exercise. Since our bodies were meant to move, he indicates, physical activity signals our cells to grow and regenerate. If we don't move, then our cells don't grow. That means our bodies begin to break down. As that happens, we experience aches, pains, and illnesses.

By becoming sedentary, our bodies begin to age and, in Dr. Lodge's terms, "decay." In fact, he indicates that keeping active helps us age as we were meant to, "slowly and remarkably well."

This information is hardly surprising to anyone who has lived in America since the 1960s, when aerobic activities began to be popular. Current books, newspapers and magazine articles regularly tout the value of exercise. There are numerous TV shows, featuring the latest health gurus, devoted to leading us through sets of exercises to help us build stronger bodies. Health club memberships are booming, and all businesses and hotels of any size have fitness rooms to help their employees and guests get moving.

The Second Master Signal

But ...the positive influence of physical activity on cells is not the most interesting finding of Dr. Lodge. Information about the *second master signal* has received less attention. And for our purpose in this book, that information is the most pertinent, and for many, the most startling.

According to his study, the second master signal to cells is equal in importance to physical activity. That other master signal is our *emotional well-being*. Dr. Lodge states, "Emotions change our cells through the same molecular pathways as exercise." He indicates that negative emotions signal our cells to stop growing while positive ones help the cells regenerate. Therefore, if we want our bodies to grow and renew, then we will exercise vigorously with all kinds of physical activities, but, *equally as important*, we will work to include positive emotions in our lives.

The beneficial emotions of optimism, joy, love, hope, and a host of other positive emotions help our cells produce new cells, according to Lodge's research. That means we may live longer and in a state of health. But just as "couch potato" living does, the negative emotions of pessimism, hate, loneliness, or despair can send signals to our cells to stop growing. When that happens, we begin to "decay" and our body ages more quickly, a process that brings death closer, says Dr. Lodge.

Common sense also tells us that emotions affect physical health. It seems vital then that we concentrate on ways to change intense negative emotions to more positive ones. It also seems important to maintain a level of positive emotions that would keep us physically healthy and emotionally fit.

Emotional Health

Our goal emotionally should never be to exist in a state of deadness, afraid to express our emotions or being concerned about ourselves if we feel deeply. Our goal is to have emotional health—all the time, not just in spurts. In other words, the goal is to be emotionally fit.

We know about physical wellness and its relationship to behaviors and habits. If we want to be physically healthy, we eat properly, exercise vigorously, take preventative measures, and promptly and appropriately take care of any physical ailment or illness. If we behave in that manner consistently, barring the contraction of a serious disease, we generally are considered to be healthy. People that are physically healthy feel good most of the time. Their bodies function well at whatever age, and they are flexible and agile. Generally, they can recuperate quickly from most illnesses and diseases.

Emotional fitness is like that. By incorporating certain behaviors, habits, and even attitudes, we can be emotionally healthy. Someone who is emotionally fit expresses feelings in non-harmful ways. The intensity and duration of their emotions are not harmful, and recovery from things that threaten emotional balance generally comes more quickly.

This book attempts to detail several of those behaviors, habits, and attitudes that can lead to a better state of emotional health. It is my belief that these behaviors, if practiced consistently, are beneficial to the one who practices them. My experience as a counselor leads me to believe that a person who displays these behaviors, habits, and attitudes regularly enjoys a healthier emotional life than one who does not do so. The one who incorporates such behaviors consistently seems to enjoy healthier relationships, appears happier, and seems to cope better with emotional upsets.

In detailing the behaviors that I think are important for emotional fitness, I have set each against a background from the ancient Scriptures. My reason for doing that is simple. This is my philosophy of life. Although many counselors may disagree, it is my firm belief that the Bible contains principles that, if followed, will lead to improvement of emotional health.

I want to make clear here, however, that while this belief forms my personal values and philosophy, it is not imposed on my clients. In fact, unless a client initiates concerns about the relationship of spiritual matters to their current difficulties, spirituality is not usually a part of our conversation.

This personal belief of mine, however, comes from two sources. First of all, it comes from my belief that the Bible is the Word of God. If that is so, which I fervently believe, then it makes sense to me that God as Creator would let His created beings know how they can have healthy, satisfying relationships and how they can cope with emotional upsets. Second, this belief has been solidified through my counseling experiences and my own life experiences. Those experiences have provided solid confirmation that God's Word contains principles for emotional health. Let's see, now, what God says about emotions.

Emotions in the Scriptures

Since creation human beings have experienced and exhibited a full range of emotions. God's holy Scriptures give realistic pictures of His people as they have both loved and hated, been angry and caring, grieved and laughed, feared and been boldly assertive, and suffered loneliness and enjoyed friends.

From the very beginning of the world, emotions have captured and controlled the hearts of man. The first couple felt *fear* and *shame* when they disobeyed God, and their son Cain, the first child born on earth, became consumed with *anger* and eventually killed his younger brother, Abel (Genesis 3 and 4). Years later, *fear* kept the ten spies sent to Canaan from believing they could conquer the land that God had promised (Numbers 13). Intense *hate* and *jealousy* filled the heart of King Saul so that he tried to kill David, the object of his envy (1 Samuel 19).

The emotion of *grief* cries to us through the pages of the Bible. Mary and Martha experienced deep grief at the loss of their brother, Lazarus (John 11); the widow of Nain mourned her only child; and both the centurion and Jairus expressed sorrow over their losses (Matthew 8; Mark 5). The profound grief of the apostles, the mother of Jesus, and even God Himself is only imagined in the understated accounts of emotions present during the crucifixion of Jesus (John 19).

All of these references indicate that emotions, no matter how mild or intense, are a part of being human. Even God's Son expressed numerous emotions in the human form he took for His life on earth. He became *angry* as He viewed commercial business being conducted in the temple (John 2). He was moved with *compassion* for the ragtag, helpless crowds that followed Him (Matthew 9). We can also imagine that He *laughed* with the children whose parents brought them to Him (Mark 10). *Fear* and *sorrow* that prompted sweat as large as great drops of blood gripped His heart in the Garden of Gethsemane as He contemplated the pain His human body would endure (Matthew 26).

Emotions were a part of the humanness of Jesus. Emotions have been and are experienced by every living person. Since God created us, and the Scriptures teach that we are made in His image, then we must conclude that God intended us to be emotional beings.

Experiencing a range of emotions only makes us human. Passion, joy, anger, disappointment, grief, and happiness flavor our lives and relationships. Without emotions, we would be nothing more than robots locked into a monotonous cycle of sameness. Arising in the morning and going about our day with no highs or lows. Tending to our work and to our relationships with no passion or intensity. How boring would that be?

Emotional Expression

Emotions themselves are neutral. They are neither positive nor negative. Having an emotion does not, by itself, harm or help. Even the intense emotion of anger, usually thought of in negative terms, does not always have a negative result. A feeling of anger is neutral.

Being angry with your spouse or kids, feeling depressed after losing a job, or even experiencing terror in the face of a threat may not be harmful, and only indicates your humanness. Emotions are not good or bad, positive or negative, helpful or harmful. The deciding factors as to whether emotions hurt or help are the expression, the intensity, the longevity, and the impact of those emotions.

A father expresses his anger by whipping his son until the child is bruised. A wife feels such intense jealousy that she questions her husband over every woman he sees. A widower does not live fully because he holds the same level of grief for years.

Because of the way the father expressed his anger, the emotion has a negative result. The intensity of the wife's jealousy may harm her marriage and endanger her own emotional health. The widower cannot see the life before him because of the intensity and longevity of his grief. Overly intense emotions held for a long time and expressed in negative ways generally impact the holder and others negatively. The ones that hold such emotions can potentially harm both themselves and others.

Physical Impact

Having intense emotions for a long period of time can impact a person physically. Much research has been conducted on the impact of negative emotions on the person who is stressed by emotions over a period of time. Stress has been linked to high blood pressure, diseases of the heart, migraine headaches, strokes, digestive problems, muscle aches and pains, as well as other ailments. It is purported that the British statesman, Enoch Powell, once noted, "When I repress my emotion my stomach keeps score." The statesman expressed what many others have experienced. Negative emotions can have a negative impact on our bodies.

Years ago I lived near a young boy who became seriously ill and was bedridden for a couple of weeks. His high fever stumped the doctors. They could not diagnosis his illness even after numerous tests. This was long before knowledge of psychosomatic illnesses (those that come about because of emotions) became common.

One doctor finally connected the dots. The boy had lost his father through a work-related accident, and, subsequently, his mother had tried to ease her grief with one male friend after another. The boy was lost and lonely. He was grief-stricken with no one to comfort him or offer him hope for the future.

His intense emotions, left unexpressed, fomented internally for months until his body rebelled. His grief, depression, and anger kept him physically ill for a lengthy period.

Spiritual Impact of Emotions

In their book, *The Cry of the Soul: How Our Emotions Reveal Our Deepest Questions about God,* Drs. Dan Allendar and Tremper Longman indicate that emotions also can have an impact on an individual's spiritual life. The authors note that we need to view emotions as to whether they "move us closer to engagement with God or move us away from greater dependence on Him." They state, "Emotions reveal how we're doing with God."[2]

The Scriptures offer numerous examples of emotions leading God's people closer to Him and, conversely, farther away from Him. Fear of the power of evil King Ahab and his queen, Jezebel, temporarily paralyzed the prophet Elijah (1 Kings 18). On the other hand, the proper fear of God can propel a person to seek a closer relationship with Him. Anger led King Saul to self destruction, but Jesus' anger propelled Him to cleanse His Father's temple.

Emotions can impact our spiritual lives. They move us forward or backward. Allendar and Longman note that the question for us as we are feeling a strong emotion might be, "Is the way I'm feeling moving me closer to God, or is it moving me farther away from Him?" We might also ask, "Will the way I'm expressing (or thinking about expressing) this emotion lead me away from or nearer to God?" If the emotion leads me farther away, then I can choose to change directions for a healthier spiritual life.

Expressing our emotions in positive ways is beneficial. Lessening the intensity of some emotions and decreasing the length of time an intense emotion is held can benefit us both physically and spiritually.

Striving for Emotional Fitness

While teaching high school and university students, I noticed that some students could accept a failing grade or criticism of a paper fairly easily, while others would have a "come apart." Some students grieved temporarily for the breakup with a girlfriend or boyfriend and then got on with their lives. Others became intensely depressed, let their grades drop dramatically, and had difficulty getting their lives back on track. For a time being, they were emotionally unwell.

I now know from clients in my counseling practice that emotional illness occurs with all ages. Most of my clients range in age from 25 years to 75 years. Just as with high school and college students, emotional fitness is a struggle for many in this age group, also. In fact, sometimes older people react to emotional stresses much as if they were teenagers.

Those same clients have taught me through the years, however, that there are certain behaviors, habits, and relationships that can lead to emotional health. In other words, by doing certain things consistently, we can come closer to being emotionally fit. I have also observed that those who have not learned these behaviors and habits or have not cultivated the appropriate relationships often have difficulty emotionally.

I have categorized these behaviors, habits, and relationships into four areas: those behaviors that need to be **confronted** to improve emotional health, ones that need to be **cleansed** from a life so a person can move closer to being emotionally fit, others that need to be **controlled** for maximum emotional well-being, and those that need to be **cultivated** to exist in a state of emotional fitness. The areas are in no particular order or ranking of importance, nor are they exhaustive. There are certainly other important ones that I have excluded. The areas chosen are simply observations from my years of teaching and counseling. I think they are important for anyone who wants to enjoy a healthy emotional life.

Let's look at the first area—confronting. This area involves two behaviors that an adult wanting to be emotionally fit needs to **confront.** One issue involves behaviors in a person's relationships that are wrong, might be wrong, or could be wrong in the future. The second is any unresolved behavior from the past that is limiting the present in some way. So, the first category discussed in this book focuses on confronting issues that need to be confronted and confronting past unresolved issues.

The second area involves two behaviors or habits a person needs to **cleanse** from his life if he wants emotional fitness. To be emotionally fit, a person needs to wash clean from his life obvious behaviors that violate his deeply held values. He also needs to wipe out an unhealthy pursuit that is prevalent in modern society. This pursuit will be explained and discussed in chapter four.

The third area is necessary for those desiring to be emotionally fit. They will need to **control** two behaviors. The emotionally healthy adult will control and maintain appropriate "fences". He will also learn to control his anger.

Last, for optimal emotional health, adults need to **cultivate** three important relationships. One relationship that needs to be cultivated is with a set of "twin" behaviors that are necessary for personal interactions to be pleasant and peaceful most of the time. These behaviors are mutually dependent and difficult to separate. Another relationship to be cultivated is with a personal support system. The third relationship to be cultivated, the most vital of all, is a personal relationship with God. This all-encompassing relationship is important for all facets of a person's life.

Let's Sum Up

Every living person is an emotional being, created to experience a wide variety of deep emotions. Emotions are neither good nor bad, but the expression of them can have either positive or negative results. Sometimes expressed and even unexpressed emotions can have physical and spiritual consequences, and, frequently, they may tell us much about our relationship with God.

Our goal then is not to be unemotional. The goal is to acquire behaviors, habits and relationships that help us to be emotionally fit, to experience deep feelings, and to express them fully in healthy, positive ways and within healthy relationships. In order to achieve emotional fitness, we may need to **confront** some behaviors, to

cleanse our lives of non-healthy actions, to **control** some habits, and to **cultivate** important relationships.

We will explore these topics in the next few chapters. In some chapters, you may recognize someone close to you. If so, you may want to give this book to that person when you have finished reading it. If you find yourself in this book, I wish you well as you work toward maximum emotional health.

Whatever the case, I wish for this book to be a blessing to each reader. My aim through this writing is to help each reader understand emotional fitness, to encourage each to express emotions appropriately, and to live a life within healthy boundaries and relationships.

For Thought and Discussion

Emotions and Health

1. What expressions of emotions have brought you the most positive results? If you are reading this in a class setting, are you willing to relate a specific demonstration of emotions and the positive results?

2. Have you ever held a negative emotion for a long time? What was the result?

3. What physical results have you witnessed from negative emotions?

4. At this early point in your reading, which of the four areas (confronting, cleansing, controlling, cultivating) do you anticipate is the most needful for you?

5. In thinking about your answer to question 4, what do you think is the basis for this being your most needful area?

PART 1

CONFRONTING

Allow motion to equal emotion
–Elbert Hubbard
Writer and philosopher

Confront What You Suspect

Chapter 1

Susan, my newest client, cried quietly as she talked about her suspicions that her husband was involved with another woman. She recounted the increasing number of nights he worked late, his distraction when he was home, and his lack of interest in sex with her. She had even found on their cell phone bill a phone number called repeatedly.

"What have you done so far about your suspicions?" I asked.

"Well, nothing," she replied. "I keep thinking that things will get better."

"Then you haven't asked him about this?" I queried.

"No, I just can't bring myself to do it," she insisted. "If it isn't true, I don't want him to think I don't trust him."

The truth is that she didn't trust her husband. He was giving her plenty of reasons not to do so, and yet she could not bring herself to ask him about it. So she remained stuck in her misery and suspicion because she was reluctant to confront a problem that couldn't be resolved until she faced it.

Susan was emotionally unhealthy during that time. She was depressed, jealous, and so consumed by her suspicions that it was affecting other areas of her life. As she talked during subsequent sessions, I learned that Susan had been emotionally unhealthy for a number of years. She outlined a variety of issues that she had not been able to face. In fact, she had developed a habit of turning away from problems and "waiting until they resolved themselves," which they seldom did.

Susan is not unique in her unwillingness to confront someone about an issue, even when there are obvious reasons to do so. Most of us have issues that crop up in our relationships that we are hesitant to face.

A friend offends us, and many of us choose to avoid the friend rather than talk with him about it. A spouse degrades us publicly, and we opt to fume and grow resentful instead of discussing it privately with him. We learn that we have hurt our best friend, and we shower her with kind words or gifts but avoid the subject of the offense. A boss treats us unfairly, and we harbor bitterness and work less passionately than before but do not mention it to her calmly or privately.

Why are we reluctant to face issues that are causing obvious distress? There are several possible reasons for reluctance to confront relationship issues, but the primary one is *fear*. We do not know what the outcome will be, and we fear it. We cannot know beforehand how the other person will react, and that can be scary. What if she gets angry? What if he leaves? What if I am fired?

Besides not knowing what the outcome will be, many simply don't know what to do. They don't know what to say or when they should say anything. They aren't familiar with problem-solving and can't separate their emotions from the issue. Often, they have become so worked up by the time a confrontation occurs that their emotions threaten to overwhelm both them and the person they are confronting.

Some people, however, just do not want to know the answers they need to know to resolve an issue. This was part of Susan's reluctance. She was afraid that she could be right about her suspicions. What if her husband confessed to an affair? What would she do then? What would happen to their family?

Learning the truth in cases like these requires action. Susan would have to *do something* if her suspicions were correct, and what she would have to do was unknown. She was understandably afraid.

When I noted Susan's reluctance that day, we talked about options. What would happen if she did nothing? She outlined a bleak picture of her current unhealthy emotional state and noted that not knowing was tearing her apart. I asked what she thought would happen if she chose other means of finding the truth, such as continuing to snoop or finding a private investigator. She noted that investigating on her own had turned up only the cell phone bill, and she could not afford an investigator. She quickly ran out of options and was left with choosing to confront her husband.

The Principle of Proactivity

Since Susan had mentioned that she was a religious person, we talked about confrontation following a principle found in the Bible. This biblical principle is *proactivity*. Proactivity is vital to those who want solid, open, and honest relationships. But what does the word *proactivity* mean? By breaking the word apart, the meaning is clearer--pro (favoring) and *activity* (acting). The word *proactivity* means becoming active about an issue or problem before it grows, taking the initiative, moving before an action is forced upon you. Being proactive is the opposite of being reactive.

Following the Principle of Proactivity allows those who practice it to solve problems and resolve issues *as they occur.* Being proactive, resolving issues as they occur, can often mean some issues never become problems in the first place. The issues are settled when they are small. Being proactive in confronting can keep issues from growing larger.

Finding the Principle of Proactivity in the Bible

The Principle of Proactivity spreads throughout the Scriptures. Jesus told his followers that even if they were at worship when they remembered that a brother had something against them, then they should be proactive about it. They should leave their worship and take care of it right then (Matthew 5:23, 24). Scriptures also teach that God's people should be proactive in helping a brother who is involved in sin, in settling a dispute with another privately, and in taking care of anger the same day it occurs (Galatians 6:1; Matthew 18:15-17; Ephesians 4:26).

These examples are crystal clear. They teach us to take the initiative to improve relationships. Resolve issues when they crop up. Take care of problems as they happen. Doing so leads us to hold each other accountable for our actions and helps us live more honest, open lives with each other. Be proactive.

Confronting suspicions early on is honest because it can stop deceit, lies and betrayal between spouses. When a husband confronts a wife who he suspects may be gambling online, he gives her the opportunity to stop lying to him about her activities. He helps her stop deceiving herself about her gambling problem. Through confronting, he cuts short her betrayal of his trust.

Confronting someone whom you have offended means the conflict can be resolved and forgiveness can be extended. Facing a

3

friend who is engaging in sinful activity can help to disentangle him from the sin and move him toward a more spiritual existence.

Confrontation is honest living. It cuts through barriers between friends and families. It exposes hidden hurt and secret sin. The honesty of confrontation demonstrates love and caring. Confrontation is proactive, and the Scriptures indicate that proactivity leads to greater spiritual health, as well as emotional health.

Caution! Not every small issue or problem needs to be confronted. Not every statement needs to be challenged. Some things are just not worth it. The things that are worth it are behaviors that erect barriers and threaten to destroy relationships and lives.

What to Confront

We have seen that confrontation can be beneficial to relationships, but specifically what kinds of things need to be confronted? For better emotional health, there are two categories of issues that need to be confronted as they occur: "wrong" behaviors and past issues that are limiting the future.

The word "wrong" has quotation marks around it because in our context the word does not necessarily mean sinful or evil. In this context it simply means that the behaviors themselves are suspicious, or that they are creating rifts in your relationships or in others' lives. They may indicate that things are just a little "out of whack," but you don't know why.

So that we can explain this better, let's further categorize the "wrong" behaviors in three ways. The ones that need to be confronted are actions that are obviously wrong, behaviors that you suspect might be wrong, or actions you notice that could be wrong in the future if they continue.

The Obviously Wrong

Behaviors that are obviously wrong are easy to identify. Confronting needs to take place when a friend has hurt you, you have offended someone, a friend is embroiled in sin, or there is abuse of any kind *(See note at end of this chapter.)* You also need to confront when there is discord with your spouse, you have an estranged family relationship or difficulties with a boss, or you are flirting with inappropriate or hurtful relationships and activities. Our society might also be improved if we personally confronted prejudicial remarks, profanity, or a lack of reverence for God as those behaviors occur.

With these kinds of behaviors, there is no doubt that an offense or estrangement has occurred. A behavior of this nature is obviously "wrong." There are other behaviors, however, that are not so easily categorized.

The Suspected Wrongs

Sometimes we are forced to confront or be confronted with behaviors that are obviously wrong because we can't escape many of them. Those actions we only suspect are wrong, however, seem to be more difficult for many of us to handle.

You need to be proactive in confronting a husband who is suddenly working late consistently or who repeatedly is not available when you call, but you can't pinpoint the reason. When a son's grades drop and his behavior does an 180° turn, it is time for a confrontation. Perhaps a friend has suddenly become cool to you and you don't know why. A co-worker has repeated episodes of what appears to be dishonesty with company funds, but you aren't sure.

You may have awakened several times this month to find your spouse is out of bed and online with the computer, and you don't know exactly what he is doing. Maybe your teenage daughter and her boyfriend give telltale signs that they might be crossing the line into sexual activity, but you are not certain. All of these instances and suspicions call for confrontation of the situation.

Ignoring suspicious behavior seldom improves it. Let me state that in another way: Ignoring behaviors that cause bells to go off in your head and "red flags" to pop up at every turn will not make the behaviors go away. In fact, time may bring about an increase of the behaviors and a worsening of the situation. Confrontation for the purpose of problem solving must take place.

Future Wrongs

Another category of "wrongs" includes behaviors that seem to be forming undesirable patterns. The behaviors may not be wrong now, but if continued, they could create major problems. These are tendencies that you notice in those you are responsible for or accountable to, or patterns of behavior that begin to develop in yourself or in loved ones that are certain to cause future difficulties.

Perhaps your spouse has had more than one episode of spending beyond your means, or one of your children seems to be drawn toward inappropriate or even dangerous friends. There may be a friend or family member that you notice has become lackadaisical about spiritual matters. Perhaps your own family is drifting toward a lack of spiritual emphasis. You may even be stopped short one day as you notice that you told a bold-faced lie without much thought.

While one action may not indicate a tendency, repeated actions over a period of time begin to form a pattern of behavior. Often the behaviors are spaced far enough apart that a pattern is not clear until the behaviors are entrenched or they begin to create difficulty. When you become aware, then it is time to confront the behavior in order to encourage and develop a more productive and spiritual pattern.

How to Confront

How do I confront? This is the million-dollar question, isn't it? Not knowing how to confront someone without creating a huge scene is what keeps most of us from any kind of confrontation.

Before confronting, however, you may need to initiate three (and sometimes four) actions to make a face-to-face confrontation easier and more productive:

- Admit to yourself that the issue exists *and* (this is the important part) *that you are going to do something about it.*
- Pray for guidance about how to bring it out in the open, pray for the necessary words to speak, and pray for the person you are confronting.
- Enlist help from others if appropriate. When you are dealing with abuse of any kind, seeking help from a professional, such as a counselor, a domestic violence agency, or the police may be necessary. At the very least, seek help from an objective, knowledgeable third party who has the ability to help you.*
- Plan what you are going to say.

Let's look at that last suggestion: Plan what you are going to say. "Aye, there's the rub," as Shakespeare's character, Hamlet, noted. What do you say? How can you be clear about the issue and communicate your feelings about it at the same time? Frequently in a confrontation, emotions take over, and the problem is not solved.

The person confronted simply responds to the emotion and not to the problem. When that occurs, the confronter and the confronted quickly move into attack-defend mode. Resolving the problem is then often forgotten.

So, anything you plan to say must include a clear picture of the actions that you are concerned about and the reasons you are concerned. *And*, (this is the key ingredient) the words need to be spoken in a problem-solving manner and not within an emotionally-laden argument. The following are suggestions for confrontations:

- Speak from love and concern, not from anger or punishment. (*I have found that people will listen to almost anything if it is said calmly and without intense, angry emotions. If emotions take over, then the listener often hears only the emotion, not the issue.*)
- Speak with an air of confidence because you are seeking to solve a problem.
- Use I statements—"I think," "I feel," "I notice," "I am concerned," etc.
- Speak of the issue and *not* the personality or character of the person. That's a sure-fire way to incite anger and cut off any problem-solving.
- Be specific. What exactly have you noticed or experienced that are causes for concern?
- Ask for explanations of the behavior. There might be a simple explanation that will ease your concerns.
- If there is no explanation given or you suspect that the explanation does not hold water, note the probable results of that behavior (or the consequences if a pattern is developing).
- Identify what specifically you want to happen or what your actions are going to be now related to the behavior. Note: *This is not a threat nor an ultimatum, only a statement that you will be alert to any like behaviors that may occur.*

Example

I'm including an example so that you can visualize what confrontations conducted in such a manner can look like. Let's suppose that you decide to confront a friend who has suddenly become cool to you. The conversation might go something like this:

"Marie, I treasure our friendship, and right now I feel a little concern because I sense there is some distance between us. I noticed that you turned your head when you saw me coming toward you last week at the ballgame, and yesterday, you talked freely with Jessica but turned away when I tried to make a comment. Have I done something to offend you, or is something else going on?"

This kind of confrontation uses the first six suggestions for confrontation. Did you notice the emphasis on "I" (the confronter) and not on "you" (the confronted)? This kind of confrontation does not accuse, which helps the confronted to listen more readily. The confrontation also includes two specific instances the speaker has noted. Then, the speaker ends with a two-part question that allows the confronted to offer another explanation.

Marie may protest mightily that you have not offended her and may offer a complete explanation of something else occurring in her life. At any rate, you have given her an opportunity to explain without assuming that she is angry with you. If she truly is angry over a real or even imagined offense of yours, then that gives you the opening to ask for forgiveness or to clear up a false assumption on her part.

That kind of conversation is honest. It opens your heart and allows for the free flow of love and concern for each other. By being proactive you might restore a friendship. At the very least, you have let the other person know that you value the friendship and want to keep it.

Let's pause here to allow an opportunity to practice this problem-solving type of confrontation. Select one of the following scenarios to practice with a friend:

a. You have found an unusually large entry on the bank statement of yours and your husband's joint account. The date of the check is the day he picked up the checkbook as he left for work. You both had recently decided not to spend over $200 without conferring first with the other. This is not the first time he has bought a large item without your knowledge.

b. Your boss cut you down verbally today in a meeting with department directors. She had approved your presentation, and it had gone smoothly, or so you thought. She is known for her cutting remarks, but this is the first time they were aimed at you. You were embarrassed in front of the managers but, more important, you felt that it was undeserved. You are confident of the accuracy of the information you included in the presentation.

c. Your son, age 20, lives with you and your husband. He graduated high school after a struggle and did not want to go to college. You assumed he would find a job, but he has made little effort. He sleeps until almost noon, hangs out with friends until late night, and continues to ask you for money. He does nothing around the house unless you specifically ask him to and seems unconcerned about his future.

How did you do? Although both you and your friend knew that this was only a practice session, could you see that confronting without intense emotions helps to solve problems? If this type of confronting is awkward for you, continue to practice until it becomes easier.

Frequently Asked Questions

The question I hear most often about confrontation is this: Won't the other person get angry? The answer to that question is "Yes, that could happen." Sometimes people who are confronted about their behavior do get angry. A follow-up question, however, is this: "What is the difference for you if the person gets angry?" The answers to that question usually indicate that most of us are afraid of another's anger.

Unless it is violent, anger is not to be feared. According to most experts, anger is a secondary emotion; that is, it is a cover for a primary emotion, such as fear, worry, guilt, or hurt. So the task for the confronter is to figure out the primary emotion. Why did the person get angry? The husband who consistently works late and is not available may get mad (secondary emotion) because of *guilt* (primary emotion). A co-worker who has committed several seemingly dishonest acts may be angry (secondary) because he *fears* (primary) for his job or because he fears what you will do with the information.

If you have confronted the person with love and concern about specific behaviors, then you have no need to fear the person's anger unless it is out of control. In his book *Love Must Be Tough*, James Dobson indicates that sometimes we have to confront and force a crisis to bring matters to a head. Even a confrontation that threatens the dissolution of a relationship, however, can be beneficial. Dobson states, "...often God uses pain and crisis to bring a sinful person to his knees."[1]

Confrontation for Emotional Fitness
Learning the art of confronting behaviors and actions that are causing difficulties can help keep you emotionally fit. By being proactive and dealing with matters as they occur, you may prevent issues from developing into major problems and, by so doing, can live in a more honest, genuine manner. Being emotionally fit requires that a person lives an open, honest, and genuine life.

* Confronting abuse is a difficult situation. Confronting an abuser may elicit more intense abuse. The way to handle many abuse occurrences is not to confront but to develop a safety plan and to leave without notice for a safe environment. Those who work with abuse situations indicate that potentially the most dangerous time for an abuse victim occurs when the victim attempts to leave. Leaving an abusive situation must be handled with the utmost care and may require intervention by professionals, such as a domestic violence agency or the police.

Questions for Thought
or Discussion

Confront What You Suspect

1. What issues are the hardest for you to confront?

2. What person or type of person is the most difficult for you to confront?

3. When you are confronted with an issue, what is your usual response? What has been the result of your response?

4. Is there an issue in your life right now that needs to be confronted?

5. What do you think is the first step you need to take to confront that issue?

This kind of forgetting does not erase memory;
it lays the emotion surrounding memory to rest.
−Clarissa Pinkola Estes

Confront Unhealthy Emotions from the Past

Chapter 2

Karleen twisted a tissue in her hands as she tearfully and hesitantly talked about her early experiences. As a very young child, she had been sexually abused by her father. The fact that she confessed this traumatic experience was a major breakthrough in our counseling work. During our last session she had hinted that a major factor in her years-long depression might be something that had happened in her past, although she did not specify.

I had suspected such an experience early on in our work together because Karleen followed the pattern of many adults who have been abused in childhood. She had no memory of her early years. "It's a black hole," she said. Until last week, she also had given no indication of any difficulties in her original family, although when she mentioned her father, her body language changed. Her shoulders tensed, and she would not maintain eye contact.

Knowing that shame and guilt follow many abused children into adulthood, I probed gently but without challenge to Karleen. If she ever told what she needed to tell, it would have to be on her terms. After all, this was her secret, one that she had kept locked in her heart since she was a preschooler. The secret had great power and had colored her opinion of herself and every decision she made for more than 35 years. She was understandably afraid of unlocking the door and letting it out.

"I'm scared," she told me. "What if I can't handle how I feel when I talk about it?" Hers was a valid question. Even thinking about the experience can evoke such intense emotions that counselors must work slowly and carefully with clients that have suffered such abuse.

> *Over the next few sessions Karleen was able finally to unburden herself of the secret. In doing so, she took the first step toward crafting a new image of herself. That new image, as an adult with power over her own life, could help her live more fully in the future.*
>
> *Karleen had been without full emotional health for years. She had let the emotions of the past determine her present life. She had hidden away such intense emotional experiences that the present was drained of the possibility of vitality and her full participation in it. In order to be emotionally fit, Karleen needed to confront the impact of the negative emotions of her past.*

The Past

Our past, if we hang on to it, has an amazing ability to control much of what we do in the present. Many past experiences carry disappointment, shock, betrayal, or destruction of innocence. Such experiences change lives in some form, and they definitely evoke intense emotions. Experiences which have occurred in childhood or adolescence can often affect us negatively even into old age if we have not successfully processed and assimilated them into the present.

Many such experiences involve an injustice of some kind. The betrayal of a friend, the infidelity of a parent or spouse, or abuse by a family member are all intense, negative experiences. Perhaps you have experienced date rape, bankruptcy or other intense financial stress, your own divorce or that of your parents, or a sudden termination from a long-held job. You may have a family member with an addiction, whether it is alcohol or drugs, sex, pornography, or the Internet. Perhaps a family member has committed a crime or is imprisoned, or a crime has been perpetrated against you. All these are emotionally charged experiences which can have the ability to impact your self-image, your decisions, and your relationships.

A Need to Confront the Past

Unfortunately for many, those emotionally charged experiences from the past are still impacting the present in a negative way. Those people may feel much as the character Holgrave describes in Nathaniel Hawthorne's *The House of the Seven Gables*, "The Past lies upon the Present like a giant's dead body." [1] Their view of themselves is sometimes so skewed by past experience that it affects every decision they make, the jobs they choose, and relationships they do or do not have. The carry-over emotions can influence their moods, their attitudes, and their interpersonal interactions.

Because their self-esteem may be low, they can be excessively dependent or independent; they may lack intimacy or be depressed. They may have difficulty loving freely; they may be bitter and lonely. Some people may be untrusting without reason, or estranged and remote from family members, or so needy that they attach themselves to the first person who offers kindness.

Perhaps the previous paragraphs describe you. If a past intense experience is limiting you by keeping you from an emotionally healthy present, then it may be time for a confrontation with that experience. Coming face to face with an experience that terrified you or robbed you of innocence may be necessary for a healthy future.

The previous statement, of course, raises questions. *Are you saying that I have to relive that experience? Why in the world would I want to relive something that caused me such intense pain?* Those are reasonable questions from anybody who has tried to deal with the results of a traumatic experience for most of his or her adult life.

Actually, that is not what I am saying. Who would ever want to relive every excruciating detail of an emotionally-charged trauma? And what person would be so cruel as to say that it is necessary to do so? The event may not need to be relived. But please note: *Sometimes even admitting to such an experience without any details can begin the path to freeing you from that experience. This is particularly true if the experience has been kept a burdensome secret.*

Secrets

Here is my reason for making those statements. Secrets based on intense negative emotions can take on a power of their own. As long as they are kept in the heart, not spoken of by a person or sometimes by a whole family, they can begin to exert control over your life. Secrets can control who you choose for friends, who you invite to your house, or what subjects you talk about with outsiders. Some secrets control whether or not you choose a mate and what kind of relationship you will have. They may control what activities you engage in, or what you do inside your house.

Secrets can be powerful. When a secret has that kind of control, the only way to take away its power is to let it loose. Letting it loose means it is no longer a secret. Thus, it loses its power.

Some families keep secret the addiction of a husband and father to alcohol. Dad's drinking may be destroying the family. It may even be associated with physical abuse. But the family does not speak of it to each other and certainly not to anyone else. Each family member suffers in silence and dreads the next alcoholic episode. Children in families like that often count the days until they can leave their home.

That secret may control who their friends are, what school activities they can engage in, and sometimes who they choose for a mate. Sometimes, girls in such a family may marry someone quickly just to get out of the house.

Another woman keeps secret her husband's addiction to pornography. She may suffer for years while her self-esteem takes a beating, and she feels undesirable and unloved. Meanwhile, her husband becomes less responsible about duties and more short-tempered. Eventually the kids want to know, "What's wrong with Dad?" But Mom does not speak of the secret to anyone, and the whole family suffers.

Others harbor the secret of childhood physical abuse. Their angry outbursts as adults may puzzle their friends or mates, and their resistance to authority may limit them in their chosen careers. But they do not whisper their secret, and so their lives are limited by experiences that may have happened decades ago.

In each of these cases, secrets about a past experience have great power over the present. Sometimes, the only way to take away that power is to tell the secret. By telling, the secret loses its ability to control your self image, your memories, and your future.

But...please note this word of caution! If you have guarded a secret that is robbing your present of vitality and life and have decided to break its control, *choose carefully the person to whom you tell your secret.* Make sure that person is trustworthy and can be objective in helping you process what has happened to you.

Often a person who has no prior knowledge of the experience may be the best one to select because of his or her objectivity. Some want to break the code of silence by talking to a family member who shared the experience with them. Sometimes that does not work well. If you try to talk with a family member, that person may not be ready to unlock the secret from her own heart. She may resist mightily, even insisting that what you remember is not true.

Remember the power of a secret and be wise in telling it. Sometimes exploring emotions can be too much for family members or friends to handle. An objective third party may be your best selection. While that person does not have to be a professional helper, she or he needs to be someone who can handle and help you to handle your intense emotions.

Letting Go of the Secret

Reliving your experience may not be necessary. *Confronting unexplored emotions* from that experience and their power over your present, however, may be vital if you want to be emotionally fit.

Two compelling reasons make confrontation of the emotions from the experience necessary, and they both are biblically based. The reasons are these: confronting gives the opportunity to practice forgiveness, and confronting keeps a person from passing on the burden to the next generation. In fact, until forgiveness is extended to those who treated you unjustly, you may not be able to find lasting peace. And knowing that you may have unwittingly passed on undesirable emotions and behaviors to your children or grandchildren may keep you from experiencing emotional peace.

Let me be absolutely clear in speaking of forgiveness: *Forgiveness is not the same as forgetting.* Only God can forgive and forget. Humans cannot. Unless you have dementia or are dead (and we are not sure about this last aspect), forgetting is impossible. God gave us memory, usually a wonderful blessing but sometimes painful. It would be ridiculous to expect anyone to forget an experience that has produced such powerful emotions.

I think many of you may be saying heatedly right now, "But (name of the offender) has not asked for my forgiveness. He/she has shown no remorse whatsoever. I don't even think they know what they have done to me." You may be correct. That person may not have a clue what they have done and how it has affected your life. Even more hurtful, if they do know, they may not care. That's a bitter pill to swallow, and that pill can keep many from seeking to learn more about forgiveness.

Robert Enright notes in the book *Exploring Forgiveness,* "Forgiveness is a special case of mercy directed at an injuring person."[2] Whether the one who treated you unjustly or caused great pain for you or your family deserves it, you can choose to forgive. You have the option to let that experience go and to break its power over you.

In fact, while forgiveness can do a great deal for the offender, it also frees the offended from bitterness, hate, and anger. To state it another way, you can choose to forgive because the other person needs it, but you can also choose to forgive for your own sake.

Another note: *Forgiveness does not necessarily mean reconciliation*. Reconciliation is not imperative for forgiveness to take place. In fact, reconciling with someone who is unrepentant may be detrimental. If you have been physically abused by an unrepentant person, you may set yourself up for continuing abuse if you try to reconcile, and bringing your own children around an unrepentant and unreformed abuser puts the children in danger.

There are other reasons that reconciliation is not always possible or desirable. The person who was unjust toward you may not be living now or may be elderly or terminally ill, or you may have no idea where that person currently lives. If that is the case, forgiveness can be given anyway, whether or not the other person ever knows.

Forgiveness releases you from resentment, anger, hurt, and despair over the offense. As long as you feel all those emotions, you are tied to the offender. As long as you hang on to the emotions, the offender is controlling your present. When you forgive, you let go of the past, of the offense, of the offender, and of the negative impact the offender made to your life. Some have expressed it as "letting go of a chain holding a two-ton anchor." What freedom is in forgiveness!

Modeling Your Life on Christ

If you are a Christian, then forgiveness becomes a sought-after way of life. Learning to forgive, whether or not others deserve it, is modeling your own life after that of Jesus. Not one of the Roman soldiers, mockers, and officials hovering around Jesus' cross deserved forgiveness, and no one asked for it. Yet He was able to pray, "Father, forgive them, for they don't know what they are doing." (Luke 23:34)

His example provides a powerful model for those who have an unjust burden laid on their hearts by someone else. Learning about forgiveness and beginning the process can be the first steps toward freedom and an emotionally healthy life.

Passing on the Burden to the Next Generation

The other compelling reason for letting go of destructive emotions or secrets is so the burden is not passed on to your children and grandchildren. Now, don't misunderstand me here. Emotions are not inherited as are the color of eyes or the upturn of a nose. But emotions can be passed on to children and grandchildren through observation and modeling of the emotions.

Let's see how that has occurred in the past through a family that may be familiar to many. The biblical account of Abraham, Isaac, and Jacob gives us a view of how a destructive pattern of behavior can be passed from one generation to the next.

Abraham

Abraham, showing a lack of faith in God's protection, practiced deception twice on journeys to Egypt and to Gerar by pretending that his wife, Sarah, was actually his sister, a half-truth at best (Genesis 20:12). Abraham was afraid that he would be harmed and his possessions would be lost.

Both Pharaoh of Egypt and King Abimelech of Gerar took beautiful Sarah into their own households, thinking she was the sister of Abraham. The deception placed in danger God's promise that Sarah would bear Abraham a son.

Isaac, Abraham's Son

In later years Abraham's son, Isaac, repeated his father's deception in exactly the same way. Isaac told Abimelech, from whom he sought refuge and help, that Isaac's wife Rebekah was actually his sister. Only the alertness of Abimelech saved this situation from disaster (Genesis 26). Although the Scriptures do not tell us, it is possible that Isaac may have witnessed his father's deception, which encouraged him to emulate the behavior.

Jacob, Abraham's Grandson

When Isaac was old, his son Jacob and Jacob's wife, Rebekah, conspired to deceive Isaac. Because Isaac's sight was poor, they dressed up Jacob as if he were his older brother, Esau. Isaac was deceived into giving Jacob the blessing that belonged to the older son (Genesis 27).

Jacob, of course, had to flee from the wrath of Esau and, perhaps Isaac, also. When Jacob returned many years later with his family, Esau met him with open arms. Jacob, however, deceived Esau once more. He told Esau they would meet again and continue the last part of his journey together. Instead, Jacob returned to his homeland by another route.

Joseph, Abraham's Great-Grandson

Deception continued to the fourth generation when Jacob's sons deceived their father into thinking that his favorite child, Joseph, was killed by wild animals (Genesis 37). With that favored child, Joseph, however, the pattern of deception was to be broken.

At the time his brothers sold him to traders, Joseph was a young man, only 17 years. He was away from his family for over 20 years. All of that time would be in a foreign country, and some of it was spent in isolation. Perhaps the separation from his family allowed him to be objective about himself and his family. Maybe the isolation caused him to meditate on actions and their consequences. Perhaps he thought about behaviors in his immediate family and in generations past.

We don't know what he thought. We do know about his behaviors, however. Those behaviors were so honest and trustworthy that the rulers in Egypt put their belongings in his care and raised him to be the governor, second in command to Pharaoh (Genesis 42:41-43).

When his ten brothers came to Egypt seeking help during a famine, Joseph did engage in a bit of deception, albeit not harmful. He could have done this to test the honesty and honor of his brothers and possibly to ensure that his father and the rest of the family would come to Egypt.

Breaking the Pattern of Deception

The most noteworthy part of this account is the way Joseph broke the pattern of deception. The record in Genesis 45 indicates that Joseph openly revealed his identity to his brothers privately and continued to do good for them. After their father died, the brothers were concerned that Joseph would try to avenge the evil that they had done to him. They expected him to be deceptive (as they had been) by only pretending forgiveness toward them while his father lived but exacting revenge after Jacob's death.

Joseph's statement, however, indicates his forgiveness and his view of the terrible injustice that had been done to him. He told his brothers, "Do not fear, for am I in the place of God? As for you, you meant evil against me, but God meant it for good..." The Scriptures record that he spoke kindly to the brothers and continued to provide for them (Genesis 50:15-21).

Note what happened: (a) Joseph revealed the truth to those who wronged him, (b) he refused to harbor anger and resentment, (c) he took a long term view of how God was able to use that injustice for good, (d) he actively forgave, and (e) he continued to do the right thing. What a beautiful picture of forgiveness and the breaking of a destructive behavioral pattern!

Let's look at that process once more. Joseph revealed the truth and refused to be bitter. He looked at the good that God was able to bring from the injustice. He then forgave and continued to do right. Joseph's actions saved God's people from extinction through starvation and helped move forward God's ultimate plan.

In the instance of Joseph and his brothers, reconciliation took place. Even if reconciliation had not occurred, however, Joseph's actions would have likely remained the same. His words indicate that he had done a great deal of thinking about his early experience. That thinking and his subsequent actions prevented the pattern of deception from being passed on to his children.

Let's note here the crucial element in breaking a negative familial pattern. The pattern of deception that had continued for generations was not broken until Joseph *forgave* his brothers. Forgiveness is the key to eliminating many destructive emotions. It is the most important ingredient in ensuring that a person does not pass on the burden of the past to future generations.

What This Means for You

You can take the same steps Joseph did. You can reveal the truth to a trusted person who can help you process it. You can refuse to harbor anger and resentment, even though the injustice generated those emotions. You can choose to forgive and work to do so, even when the offender does not deserve it. You can look for ways that God has been able to use your experience to bring about good in your life, and you can continue to do good and right things.

I urge you to confront experiences from the past that are having a detrimental effect on the present. Work through them with a trusted, loving and compassionate person. Refuse to let those experiences have control over your life. Memorize Romans 8:28 and let that guide the long-term view of your experiences. Begin and complete the process of forgiveness.

Confront emotionally traumatic experiences of your past. Make sure those experiences have been accepted for what they were, emotions have been resolved, forgiveness has been extended, and secrecy has been exposed. It takes a great deal of courage to go through that process. Not everyone can do it, but if you are able to do so, you are moving closer to being emotionally fit.

For Thought and Discussion

Confront Unhealthy Emotions from the Past

1. What issue from your past is negatively impacting your present?

2. Have you ever told anyone about that past issue? If so, what was the person's reaction?

3. Are there events happening in your life now that might negatively impact your children's future lives?

4. If there are such events, can you be experiencing burdens that have been passed on from a previous generation? If you do not wish to pass on the burden, could forgiveness be an option for you? How would that be accomplished?

5. To what person(s) would you be most likely to reveal a personal secret that has negative impact on your life? How has that person proven to be trustworthy with other secrets? What about that person leads you to believe he or she can help you with the outcome of your secret?

PART 2
CLEANSING

There can be no happiness if the things
we believe in are different from the things we do.
—Freya Stark

Cleanse Your Life of Deliberate Violations

Chapter 3

Ben, stoic and ill at ease, sat stiffly in the wing chair in my counseling office. I had just asked his wife Carol, the occupant of the other chair, to step out to the reception area so that he and I could talk for a few minutes. Carol, pretty and petite but obviously at her wits' end, had come to see me alone for the first session to talk about their marital difficulties. Both of them were here now for the second session, and although we tried diligently to narrow their issues and develop counseling goals, we seemed to be going in circles. Ben had had little to say during the first part of the joint session and was obviously uncomfortable for he sat with the upper half of his body turned slightly away from Carol.

When he and I were alone, I asked bluntly, "Ben, what is really going on here?" After hemming and hawing for a few minutes, he finally stated he just didn't love Carol any more. Acting on a suspicion, I asked as gently as possible, "So who do you love?" He stared intently at me for a while and then bowed his head and covered his face with his hands. "You won't tell Carol, will you?" he mumbled.

Ben spent the next 15 minutes telling me about his nine-month affair with a woman he had met through work. The affair had confused him about his loyalties and love and turned his beliefs and values about marriage upside down.

His part of our discussion, as is usual in these cases, largely consisted of contradictory statements and his conclusion that Carol and their children would be fine after a short period of adjustment. In other words, this incident in their lives would create only a wrinkle for a while but would have little long-term effect, or so he thought. By telling him what research has

> shown about the effects of family breakups and what my personal and counseling experiences indicated, I gave him a different perspective.
>
> The truth is that Ben had violated some of his deepest values. As a strong believer in God's Word as truth, he had violated one of God's primary commandments. He had voluntarily chosen to engage in an emotional and sexual relationship with someone other than his wife. This affair had the potential to wreck his marriage, estrange his family, create difficulties at work, and endanger his soul. Ben was in sin.
>
> Sometime later at my urging, Ben finally confessed his affair to Carol, who understandably was devastated. At some point, the fog in his head cleared a little, and he decided that spiritually and emotionally he did not want to be where he was. He asked for and received help from a respected church member to try to get his spiritual life back on track. He and Carol and I spent hours during several months working to heal their marriage.

The Effects of Deliberate Sin

Sin is like that, confusing and playing havoc with our values and beliefs and even our common sense. Choosing to engage in a deliberate sin usually doesn't stop there. It also expands to include other sins. Ben's choice to engage in an affair led him to lying, deception, abdication of his roles as husband and father, neglect of extended family and work, and destructive anger when questioned about his actions.

Interestingly those engaged in a deliberate sin often state that they have never felt more alive, more open to the world. This "aliveness," however, frequently refers to their heightened senses as they continually try to dodge being caught. It also generally indicates a letting go of moral restraints and an awakening of their sensual, lustful natures.

I have observed that most moral, godly people who are caught up in a sin are actually far from "alive." Until the sin clouding his life was completely gone, and he was reconciled with both his God and his family, Ben did not recognize he had been miserable during the time of his sin. His misery showed in every aspect of his being–clouded thinking, estrangement and isolation, withdrawal from normal activities, and numbness of emotions. It even showed in his body language by halting subdued speech patterns, stoic facial expressions, and flat affect. Ben was in an emotionally unhealthy state.

How Does a Person Get into Sin?

An obvious question is, "How does someone get to the point of voluntarily making a choice like that? A choice that leads to misery and perhaps loss of morals, family, and other things that one holds dear?"

Ben got into sin just the way most of us do--through the "Boiling Frog" process. As the old story goes, plop a frog into boiling water, and he will jump out quickly. But put him into a pot of cold water, turn up the heat slowly, and he will be boiled before he knows it.

Sin seems to work like that. It sneaks up on us. It starts slowly and begins steadily to work on our thoughts. It begins as a repeated whisper in our ear that twists our thoughts, and then it becomes a louder voice wearing us down before its shout shakes our soul.

The Scriptures give a clear indication of the process of the ensnarement of sin in Psalm 1:1. The phrase "walks...in the counsel of the wicked" indicates that the words of those who are immoral can have great effect on those of us who must live among them. If we choose the ungodly for our close friends and associates, then their words carry a great deal of weight. Sometimes idle statements uttered over time by friends like that cause us to question our own beliefs and open us to a more immoral view of the world.

If we listen to the advice of the wicked, we often begin to want to be around them more often, to be more like them and to engage in their activities. We then begin to "stand in the way of sinners." They become our close friends. We don't want to be different from our friends, so we begin to like what they like, talk the way they do, and think as they think.

After enough time has passed in this way, many of us let go of our moral inhibitions altogether and even begin to "sit in the seat of scoffers." We may finally come to the point where we, too, scoff at God and His laws. Through urging of friends, we begin to think and act contrary to our earlier values until finally, sin has dominance over our lives. The progression from the "counsel of the wicked" to "sitting in the seat of the scoffers" is a slow process but deadly. Over time the frog is boiled.

Interestingly, the same verse in Psalms indicates that the person who does not succumb to that process is the happy (blessed) one.

Verse 2 in that chapter indicates that real happiness comes to the person whose "delight is in the law of the LORD, and on his law he meditates day and night." The two verses following note that such a person is stable and productive. In other words, he is emotionally fit. So, continually cleansing our lives of obvious sins is essential if we wish to have emotional health.

Choices

Much of the tenor of our lives consists of the choices we make day to day. To illustrate, look at any of the following choices and predict the probable outcome: calling to apologize to a person with whom we have had a strained relationship; choosing gentleness over harshness in dealing with a family member; choosing to do our jobs when others are malingering; choosing to go out with friends when our husband doesn't want us to; choosing to leave a lunch because the gossip is juicy; choosing to go out "clubbing" with a close friend on the weekend; choosing to respond to a flirtatious email; sneaking out with a girl that your parents don't approve of; choosing to follow up on a sexy comment from a co-worker of the opposite sex; choosing to leave home because "life just isn't fun anymore."

Choices of this nature, made daily, can have positive or negative results. A series of unwise choices can lead to a sinful life. When Ben, the husband in the first of this chapter, made the initial choice to have close personal contact with a female co-worker, he stepped toward a life of sin. His daily choices after that--to phone her, to invite her to lunch, to have long conversations, to text her numerous times a day, to meet after work, to visit her home, to talk about his home life with her--led him deeper and deeper down the path until he was fully engaged in an immoral relationship with her. As in Psalm 1:1, he first walked, then stood, then sat in the midst of immorality.

David's Choices

Although he was "a man after God's own heart," King David made a series of unwise choices in his life. Those choices led him to adultery, deception, and the murder of an innocent man. He became embroiled in sin, which resulted in the death of his child and his own estrangement from God.

Chapter 11 of 2 Samuel gives a clear picture of David's choices. The chapter opens with an interesting statement, "In the spring of the year, the time when kings go out to battle...David remained at Jerusalem." David was the king. He should have been leading his troops, but he made an unwise choice. Instead of leading his army in their battles, he sent Joab and his servants and "all Israel." Something was clearly wrong. David was the leader of Israel, but he abdicated his role and let someone else take over for him. That was the first choice that led him on a downward spiral into sin. He was not focusing on the job he needed to do.

Second, in contrast to his troops who were camping in the open field, David was living leisurely and appeared to become restless (v 2). In this leisure and restlessness, he evidently couldn't sleep. He walked on the roof in the evening and observed a woman bathing. David could have chosen quickly to turn away, to engage himself in healthy pursuits, or to get on with the business of the kingdom, but he did not. Evidently, he looked at this woman named Bathsheba long enough to note that "she was very beautiful." Looking too long ("standing in the way of sinners") led him one step closer to overt sin.

Choices came faster for David after that. He chose to inquire about the beautiful woman and learned that she was the wife of one of his soldiers. He then chose to call for her for a sexual relationship. Let's get the full picture: A Commander-in-Chief sought out the wife of one of his soldiers who, at the time, was fighting battles for the Commander. While the soldier was gone from home, the Commander-in-Chief had a sexual relationship with the soldier's wife. Most of us would say that is despicable behavior. Many sins result in despicable behavior.

When Bathsheba later told David she was pregnant, the king chose to call her husband Uriah home from battle so that Uriah would lie with his wife and David's sin would be covered. But David did not count on Uriah having more honor than he himself had. Uriah refused to enjoy the pleasures and luxuries of home when all his fellow soldiers were in terrible conditions in the field. David then chose to get Uriah drunk so that he would go home. But Uriah still chose the honorable way. He did not go home.

David then made the unthinkable choice to have Uriah killed in battle. He arranged with his commander of troops, Joab, to put Uriah in the heat of battle and withdraw from him, leaving Uriah alone to defend himself against many. Uriah died as a result. David, the great leader of God's powerful Israelite army, had chosen to kill one of his own soldiers rather than face his own sin. What a cowardly, despicable act for a commander in chief!

David had become awash in sin. He had walked, then stood, then sat in the midst of sin. He even became one of the scoffers (2 Samuel 12:9, 14). David stayed that way for a period of time. He was an unrepentant sinner until his secret sins were exposed publicly by God through the prophet Nathan. Nathan confronted David face to face.

In the book of Psalms, David gave us a glimpse of what his emotional state was during his time of sin. He noted that when he kept his secret in silence, his bones "wasted away through my groaning all day long" (Psalm 32:3). He felt that God's hand was heavy on him and that his strength "was dried up as by the heat of summer" (v 4). In other words, David was an emotional wreck. Sin had made havoc of David's emotional health. Even after his sin was exposed, and repentance and reconciliation with God had occurred, he stated that his sin was on his mind constantly (Psalm 51:3).

A Central Choice for Everyone

Joshua, another great leader of the Israelites, indicated in his speech upon their taking over the land of Canaan, that we all have a central choice to make (Joshua 24:15). Joshua gave the people a brief accounting of how God had planned long ago to bring the Israelites to the land of Canaan and help them conquer it. He then told the people what they should do: "...fear the Lord and serve him in sincerity and in faithfulness" (v. 14). After all, their God had cared for them and dealt with them justly. He had fulfilled his promises to their father Abraham to make them a great nation and to give them a land of their own. This God deserved nothing less than their loyalty and faithfulness.

Joshua then asked the people to make a conscious choice. They should choose to follow the gods of the people around them, or they should choose to follow God (v 15). No divided loyalties. They had to make a choice. Joshua then made that bold and wonderful statement of his own choice, "But as for me and my house, we will serve the LORD."

Each one of us faces that central choice at some point in life. That one choice then should be the governing force for all the daily choices for the rest of life. Unfortunately, sin is powerful and frequently pulls us away from the path of truth and light. The only way back is to begin making choices consistent with that central life choice.

A Choice of Roads

Although there is no indication the poet had in mind any religious connotation, Robert Frost's poem, "The Road Not Taken," illustrates the importance of the choices we make. A traveler came upon two paths leading into the woods. He took one of them. He wanted to save the other for another time, but doubted even then that he would come back because "way leads onto way."

He ends the poem by describing how he will look back when he is older and tell about these two paths. The last line does not indicate what kind of consequences he enjoyed or suffered, but it does describe the end result of his choice of path: The road he took has "made all the difference."[1]

As does Frost's traveler, each time we choose we move farther down one way or another. Often, when we have gone so far, even if we desire to go back, the way to do that seems almost impossible.

The Effects of Wrong Choices

Several years ago at a gathering, I saw a former student who had been in a senior English class I had taught years earlier. We had not seen each other since his graduation 20 or 25 years before. As a high school student, he had been smart but boisterous, lively, and frequently in trouble with his teachers for childish mischief. He was a Christian, and I had loved his energy and enthusiasm for life.

As we chatted on that evening many years later, I couldn't help but note his subdued manner and the pain and sadness in his eyes. While we caught up on the intervening years, he told me the reason for his pain—it centered on the choices he had made in those intervening years. He had moved out of state not long after graduation, goofed off during college but managed to get his diploma and eventually worked at a sales job he loved. That job had ended recently because of his choice to become entangled in an unethical deal.

He had married a gentle, pretty young woman he met in college. As we talked, he said, "I have lost her because I chose to become involved with another woman." He no longer had a close relationship with any of his three children because he had hurt their mother and betrayed their trust. He even admitted that through their childhood, he had chosen consistently to spend too much time at work and neglect them. "In short, my life has become a mess," he said. He went on to describe how emotionally unhealthy he had been as a result of all his choices to engage in sin.

My heart broke for the unfulfilled promise he had shown as an 18-year-old and for the youthful energy and hope that he might never have again. I asked, "What do you intend to do now?" To that, he gave a most surprising answer. He looked me squarely in the eyes and stated emphatically, "I wanted to come back where I started, see if I could connect with who I used to be, and choose differently this time."

Although he couldn't ever erase the consequences of his earlier choices to engage in sin, he wanted to make a fresh start and deliberately choose wisely this time. He had once made a central choice. He had chosen God, but his ensuing choices had led him away from godly things.

I wish I could tell you that his life is different now, that he and his family have reconciled, and he is a productive worker, but I don't know any of that. We lost touch and I don't know what has happened to him. I pray for him and others like him whose lives are in a mess because they have chosen to engage in deliberate sin.

That former student stood daily at a fork in his path. He could choose the road to do right or not. He had chosen not to do right so many times that he had gone far from his real nature, ignored his values, and left God. All he wanted was to come back to the beginning of the path and make the right choice.

My friend's life reminds me of the song, "Slow Fade," recorded by Casting Crowns. The song describes what happens when a person continually compromises his own values. The lyric writer notes that over time there is a slow "crumble" as the person loses himself piece by piece.[2]

A choice to be involved in sin leads to disease in the heart, the seat of our emotions. Going against our deeply-held values and our conscience does not lead to emotional health. If you want to be emotionally fit, then it is imperative that you cleanse your life of deliberate violations of your deeply-held values.

For Thought and Discussion

Cleanse Your Life of Obvious Wrongs

1. Have you ever made a choice that led you off the spiritual path? If so, what effects did it have on you and on your family?

2. Have you ever observed another person's life when he or she has made a series of unwise choices? What were the effects of those choices?

3. What, if anything, do you do to keep yourself from making unwise choices?

4. What are your suggestions for those who want to change the "slow fade" that has come from their unwise choices?

5. What are the difficulties that face people who want to change their wrong choices to better ones?

Cleanse Your Life of Unhealthy Pursuits

Chapter 4

Through the years of my counseling practice, numerous clients have explained to me what they think God wants for their lives. Marlene was such a client. She had just detailed what had been going on in her life, how her husband was not meeting her needs, how her children were difficult, and how her job was unsatisfactory.

She explained that a few months ago, her co-workers, who seemed to be a happy lot, had invited her to go partying with them after work. Although reluctant at first, she finally caved in and found after a few times that she was "having more fun than I have ever had before." In fact, she had met a man during one of their forays who "was on my wavelength and seemed to know what I was thinking." They had grown close in the last few weeks. She was now thinking seriously about leaving her husband to live with this man.

The fact that she was in my office indicated she was confused about this choice. She talked for several minutes about how the choice would be difficult for her family, but then she blurted with copious tears, "I know God wants me to be happy!"

Marlene was just the latest in a series of clients who had made that same statement. Some clients thought they were being denied happiness because they were in a low-paying job. If they could only find a job that matched their inflated opinion of their own skills, they would surely be happy.

Others thought that success had eluded them and thus happiness had, also. No ordinary job had satisfied them because they wanted to accomplish some great goal so others would applaud and envy them. They would then be happy.

A number of clients thought that they had found the one person in the world with whom they could be happy. Their own spouses and children had not brought them the happiness each felt he or she deserved. But if they could only be with this person "who totally understands me," then they would be happy.

All of these clients had in common one pursuit—the pursuit of happiness. They knew without a doubt that God wanted them to be happy. They were on a lifetime pursuit of an emotional feeling they equated with happiness. For many, pursuing happiness meant chucking everything that was in their lives presently—family, job, church—and following that will-o'-the-wisp called happiness.

Were they correct? Would they find happiness? What exactly is happiness? Does God want us to be happy? And, with the definition given by these clients, does being happy mean a person is emotionally healthy? We will look at those questions in this chapter. First, however, let's look at the routes to happiness, according to our current culture.

Culture's Pursuits

Our society views happiness as a worthwhile pursuit and continually gives us pictures through print and visual media about what will bring that about. If we have wealth, or success, or power, we will be happy. If we are in the "right" relationship, we will feel happiness. And if we have a variety of fun-filled activities that entertain and bring pleasure, then surely we are happy. Yet, society tells a falsehood.

Wealth

While wealth can be useful for accomplishing much good, it does not bring happiness. The late Howard Hughes, one of the wealthiest men in the world during his time, lived as a recluse in his later years. He had such a phobia about germs that anyone who came into his presence had to wear gloves and a mask. His wealth had not brought him happiness. He died an unhappy, isolated, and emotionally unhealthy man.[1]

Success

Almost every person wants to feel that he has achieved some measure of success. The problem, however, with success equated with happiness is this: what is success? If we were to ask ten people to define success, ten differing definitions would tumble forth. Success to some is rearing children who are productive and charitable citizens. Success to others is achieving some goal in their careers. Some think that success is using one's talents for good. Others think fame or wealth is success. So the term *success* is nebulous and individually oriented. How can happiness come from success if we cannot define success?

Most of us would have called Richard Nixon successful. He had started life in a small farmhouse on his parents' lemon ranch. When he later was elected to the office of President of the United States, he became the most politically powerful man in the world. Yet, he died a disgraced man, the President who resigned rather than face criminal charges.

Numerous athletes and entertainers have reached the pinnacle in their careers, but they run through relationships like they do through a handful of M&Ms and their misdeeds make front-page headlines. Those athletes are considered successful in their careers, but stable relationships elude them.

Others, who according to their own definition are "successful," live unhappy lives. They may have reared good children, or reached the pinnacle in their chosen career fields, or given themselves in service to their country or to philanthropic ventures, but they are miserable because of other factors impacting their lives. So, "success" as defined by many in our culture does not always bring happiness.

"Right" Relationships

All of us would like to be in a loving, mutually beneficial relationship with a mate. Yet searching and finding the "right" relationship will not bring us happiness. We all know those who are in good marriages and yet are not happy. Perhaps their children cause problems or their jobs are unfulfilling, or their health has failed, or they are burdened with the care of elderly parents, or they face a host of other issues. While a solid, warm relationship with a loving partner can go a long way toward helping us have a pleasant *feeling,* it does not guarantee happiness.

Fun

In the last few decades, the pursuit of fun has seemed to be the number one way by which many hope to find happiness. Millions of dollars are spent on games, toys, drugs, and entertainment. While relaxing and having some fun are essential for our emotional well-being, today there seems to be a hot pursuit of anything that can give a moment of pleasure.

In a 2008 magazine article, the talented actor Robert Downey, Jr., told how he spent years pursuing a life of pleasure, with drugs and alcohol. He was known as a party boy, and his bouts with the law were well known. He stated, "I thought my way was so much cooler than people who were actually building lives and careers."

After years of being in and out of jail and rehabilitation facilities, something clicked for him. For the past several years, he has been sober and hard-working. He now says, "I used to be so convinced that happiness was the goal, yet all those years I was chasing after it, I was unhappy in the pursuit." He concludes, "Maybe the goal really should be a life that values honor, duty, good work, friends and family." [2]

So, if all these things that society views as bringing happiness prove not to do so, then how do we find it? And, besides that, is happiness itself even a worthwhile goal?

Do We Have a Right to Happiness?

Before we begin to discuss those questions, we need to look at another more basic question: Do we have a God-given right to happiness? Many people think we do. After all, the American Declaration of Independence firmly states that all men (people) have been endowed by their Creator with inalienable rights to "life, liberty, and the pursuit of happiness." In fact the document notes that this is a self-evident truth.

While the Declaration of Independence is a marvelously-written document from visionaries who laid the foundation for a system of government in America, the writers were only human, not divine. This document spells out for its citizens what the founders intended every citizen to have—freedom to live as they wished within the confines of law.

While America's founding fathers felt that pursuing happiness was the right of every person, is that really a God-given right? Is happiness God's greatest desire for man?

What Does God Say about Happiness?

Let's answer this question by searching the Scriptures to see what God says about happiness. The word *happy* or *happiness* is conveyed by the biblical term *blessed,* although the word *blessed* has other connotations as well. Read the following verses that contain the word *blessed* to get an idea of what brings happiness:

> Psalm 106:3
> Psalm 112:1,2
> Psalm 119:1,2
> Psalm 128:1,2
> Psalm 144:15
> Psalm 146:5

After careful reading, it becomes abundantly clear that, according to God, worldly pursuits will not bring happiness. Let's look at those verses again to see how God defines a happy person:

Psalm 106:3	one who "does righteousness at all times"
Psalm 112:1	one who "fears the Lord"
Psalm 119:1,2	one who "walks in the law of the Lord," who keeps His testimonies," and who "seeks Him with the whole heart"
Psalm 128:1,2	one who "fears the Lord" and "walks in His ways"
Psalm 144:15	one "whose God is the Lord"
Psalm 146:5	one who "has God for his help" and "whose hope is in the Lord"

We can see from these verses that the person who seeks God, obeys Him, and lives righteously according to His laws is the truly *blessed* or happy person. That person may not be wealthy or successful or even fun. In fact, that person may be poor, unknown outside a small circle of family and friends, and have no time or money for fun pursuits. *But...*Scriptures indicate if that one walks with God daily and lives righteously, he is blessed by God. He is happy.

The New Testament also helps us see the attributes of a blessed or happy person. In His Sermon on the Mount, Jesus gave a listing of characteristics of those blessed by God (Matthew 5:3-10). He said that happy (*blessed*) people are humble, self-controlled, righteous, merciful, pure, peace-making, and even reviled for following Him.

These qualities are quite the opposite of the qualities that our culture appears to attribute to powerful, successful people. In the eyes of many in our society, a powerful, successful person would be self-assured and assertive, a doer and goer who often likes the spotlight. He would most likely not be humble, peace-making, merciful, and self-controlled. Yet God said the humble person is the one who is happy.

Conclusions

So after looking at the Scriptures, discussing the kinds of things that bring real happiness, and noting the qualities of one who is blessed by God, what can we conclude? Is the pursuit of happiness a worthwhile goal? Does a right relationship matter? Does being happy mean that we must not be wealthy, successful, or enjoy life? What can we conclude about happiness?

Conclusion 1

Our culture is correct in that true happiness does come from a right relationship. However, the right relationship is not the union of one human heart with another human heart. It is not finding a mate that you love and with whom you want to spend the rest of your life, although that can be a good thing for you. The right relationship is the one you have with God. That's where happiness resides. Happiness begins when you seek to know the heart of God, to learn about Him, and to obey His voice and will.

Conclusion 2

Happiness is not the goal of life. The pursuit of happiness is not the goal. In fact, the more you pursue happiness, the less likely you are to find it. It cannot be found by looking for it, for happiness is a by-product of another pursuit. Happiness comes when you are not looking for it. It comes when you are earnestly engaged in something else. That something else is the pursuit of a life with God. Nathaniel Hawthorne once noted, "Happiness in this world, when it comes, comes incidentally. Make it the object of pursuit, and it leads us a wild-goose chase, and is never attained. Follow some other object, and very possibly we may find that we have caught happiness without dreaming of it."[3]

Happiness is a serendipitous quality. You find it while you are on your way somewhere else. When you are engaged in worthwhile spiritual pursuits, work and unity with God, happiness often comes incidentally. You are actively pursuing a life dedicated to God, and suddenly, there it is. You may wake up one day and realize that your life, while not wealthy, successful in a worldly sense, or even fun, is a happy one. You have a mission, a work to do, and a solid relationship with your Creator.

So since happiness is a by-product of another pursuit, it is useless to search for it. Until your life has the right foundation and goal, happiness is absent. Until your efforts are spent living for Him, real happiness will not come.

Conclusion 3

You and I can be happy if our lives are lived for God. The amazing thing is that if we do so, we will ultimately have all the things the world values. Now, don't misunderstand me here. We may still never have more than $100 in the bank at one time. We may never serve in the top position of our company, and our lives may not have much laughter and entertainment. But a life with God gives us *spiritually* everything the world deems worthy of pursuit. Isn't that mind-bending?

You see, by seeking a close relationship with God, we don't give up anything. In fact, spiritually we gain wealth, success, and relationships. We don't lose, we gain, and we gain more than we can ever imagine. Jesus told His followers, "I have come that they may have life, and that they may have it more *abundantly*" (John 10:10). He gives His followers an abundant life, filled with good.

We Gain Spiritual Wealth

Many value *wealth* and think that happiness comes from it. But Jesus tells us to "lay up treasures in heaven" where they can't be destroyed or stolen. That's quite an investment plan. The more we live for Him here, the more treasures we will have there. We can be incredibly wealthy spiritually both here and hereafter.

We Gain Spiritual Success and Power

Many think that happiness comes from *success and power*. God will give both success and power spiritually. If you love and obey God, you will receive a crown at Judgment and hear Him say to you, "Well done, good and faithful servant. You have been faithful over a little; I will set you over much" (Matthew 25:21). A large number of people may never know your name on earth, and you may never win earthly rewards, but you can have a spiritual crown for eternity.

The humblest, meekest person on earth who follows God faithfully has great power. That person may never rule nations or make daily decisions that affect thousands, but he can be one of the most powerful people on earth because of God's presence in his life. Paul tells Timothy that God gave His followers a "spirit not of fear but of *power* and love and self control" (2 Timothy 1:7).

Paul also notes that God is able to do so much more than we can even think or imagine, "according to the *power* at work within us" (Ephesians 3:20). He makes clear what that power is when he says, "...it is God who works in you both to will and to work for his good pleasure" (Philippians 2:13). What an extreme measure of power to have the Creator of the universe working within us!

How I Answer Now

How do I answer now when a client who has spent his life following God tells me that God wants him to be happy by doing something sinful? I say, "You are absolutely right. God does want you to be happy." Then we spend quite a bit of time on what the client thinks happiness is and what values are important to him. We also review any violations of those values and the ensuing results. Usually the person must make a choice. Will he choose to engage in the wrong behavior that he desires and find a life of confusion and anguish, or will he choose to follow God's ways and find real happiness?

If he chooses to continue sinning, then real happiness will elude him. In just a short while, he may find that his life is off track, his emotions are on a roller coaster, and he can't find happiness no matter where he looks.

A sinful life will not bring true happiness. There may be moments of pleasure, of laughter, of love, and even of some contentment, but there will not be the deep-in-the-center-of-the-soul joy in who you are and what you do. That can only come from a godly life lived in obedience to the Creator. After such a life, not only will you receive a crown, but you will hear, "Enter into the *joy* of your master" (Matthew 25:21).

This kind of happiness is worthy of pursuit. So, if you have been chasing after earthly happiness, cleanse your life of such an unhealthy pursuit and give everything you have to pursuing a life with God. Only then can genuine and lasting happiness be yours, and only then can you be on the path to real emotional health.

For Thought and Discussion

Cleanse Your Life of Unhealthy Pursuits

1. If someone described you as successful, how would you interpret that?

2. Think of five happy times in your life. Do those times share a common ingredient?

3. Has there ever been a time when you pursued something that you thought would bring you happiness, but it didn't? What was the reason that it did not?

4. Which of society's pursuits of happiness (wealth, power, success, fun, relationships) have you observed most often in the lives of those around you?

PART 3
CONTROLLING

Control Your Fences with Two Responsibilities

Chapter 5

"My life is out of control!" Kailey declared with feeling, after detailing all the obligations and daily chores she must do for a "demanding" husband, three "selfish" children, and a boss who treated her "like I don't have good sense." She described her current emotions as "angry, frustrated, and bedraggled."

"And it seems I can never please anybody," she noted. "The more I try to do all the things they want and ask for, the worse I feel."

Kailey's life really was out of control. That is, her life was out of her control, but it was being well controlled by those with whom she spent the most time. Kailey was a kind and caring wife, mother, and employee trying to do the right things. She felt that to ask, and in some cases demand, that others consider her needs was somehow not "Christian."

Kailey's feelings are shared by many. Their families, co-workers, and friends keep them running to meet the demands of home, workplace, and sometimes even church. If those family members and friends don't have time or the will to do their own tasks, they often think of someone like Kailey. "Kailey will do it," they say because Kailey has stepped in so often before to perform their tasks.

Friends and family members who make a statement such as that do not have malice in their hearts. They do not intend to harm or to make life difficult for women like Kailey. They would probably be deeply concerned if they knew of the deep resentment and hidden anger that Kailey and others like her harbor. They might even state, "Why didn't she say something? I didn't know." That is precisely the case. They do not know

> *because people like Kailey do not tell them. In short, others take advantage of them because they allow it.*
>
> *Such individuals as Kailey are usually kind-hearted and giving, but misguided. They spend much time in simmering resentfulness without knowing the reason. Their own needs are pushed aside so the needs of others can be met. They often feel overworked and underappreciated.*
>
> *When I asked Kailey to describe how she felt as others continually asked her to do jobs they could do themselves, she stated, "I feel like they don't even see me. They don't ask whether I have time or want to do whatever it is. It's like I'm not even there or certainly not important." When I asked if she could remember ever saying to them that she didn't have the time or didn't wish to do something, she frowned as if this was a new concept and whispered, "No. I would feel so guilty if I did."*

Those who share Kailey's experiences do not pay much attention to their own emotions or needs. Although they know they feel angry and resentful, they cannot seem to equate those emotions with the inability to say *no* to others. Kailey had come to see me because she wanted to know how to manage her time better. She did not recognize that time management was not the central issue. The central issue was that she had allowed others to cross over her own natural boundaries.

She and others like her have not learned the appropriateness of having healthy fences around them. Their unhealthy emotions, however, are giving them daily indications that for their own emotional health, they need to rebuild and control those personal barriers. Kailey actually might have needed to learn to manage her time better, but her primary need was to be emotionally fit. To do that, she would have to learn what her fences were, how to communicate those fences to others, and what she needed to do to rebuild them when they were violated.

Two Principles*

The subject of appropriate fences is one of vital importance in maintaining emotional health. Numerous books have been written about the subject. Henry Cloud and John Townsend's excellent book *Boundaries* is one of the first that brought this to the attention of the public and gives much more detailed information than we can cover in these chapters.

While the term *boundary* illustrates well the concept, I have chosen the word *fence* because of two extra qualities that the word *fence* conveys: A *fence* is easier to visualize for some people since it is an actual object, and most fences are transvisual**, i.e. you usually can see through them from both sides (chain link, rail, wrought iron, picket fences, etc.). This last concept illustrates that emotional fences are not meant to be impenetrable barriers to hide behind. Fences are meant to differentiate between what belongs to you and what belongs to another, but they also allow you to see each other and communicate with each other freely.

Because of the numerous clients I have had with difficulties in this area, I think this subject is so important that we are devoting two chapters to the idea. In this chapter we will discuss two biblical principles (also mentioned by Cloud and Townsend among others). I have specified these two principles because I think they are essential for understanding the concept of fences and need to be emphasized. We will also look at a few concrete ways these principles play out in our lives. The next chapter indicates practical ways of using the two principles in deciding what fences are appropriate for our own lives and communicating that information to others. Finally, we will also discuss three frequently asked questions about fences at the end of the second chapter.

Individual Responsibility

The first principle important to the understanding of emotional fences is that of *Individual Responsibility*. This principle is found throughout the Scriptures. Several passages (Romans 14:10-12; 2 Corinthians 5:10; Galatians 6:4, 5) tell us plainly that *each one* of

---

* *One of the two principles is actually a natural law, but for the purpose of this and the next chapter, we will treat both as principles.*

***The word transvisual does not appear in nine online dictionaries, so I am assuming that it is my own invention, at least in this context.*

us is responsible for our own work on this earth, and each will be judged individually.

The concepts found in Ezekiel 18:19, 20 clearly illustrate that each adult is responsible for his own behavior and deeds. Our parents, our children, our spouses cannot answer for us, nor are their deeds our responsibility. We are not responsible for someone else's behaviors and choices, whether it is an adult child or a parent (as in this passage), a spouse, a co-worker or a friend.

The principle that an individual is responsible for his own behavior, thoughts, and deeds permeates the Bible. This is an important principle which we will reference often throughout these two chapters. Remember: *The Principle of Individual Responsibility.*

Sowing and Reaping

The second principle (law) is that of S*owing and Reaping.* This law of nature is easily illustrated throughout the natural world. Any farmer or gardener understands the principle well. If you sow petunia seeds and the conditions are favorable, you will have a bed of petunias in due time. If you sow corn in the garden, then corn stalks soon appear. Pigs produce other pigs and horses produce horses. This is an unchanging law of God's natural world.

We even understand this principle as it applies to our daily behavior. If we want friends, we know we must sow friendly gestures, friendly talk, and friendly behaviors. Those who have sown kindness and gentleness in their families reap the same from family members.

God tells us not to deceive ourselves about this principle (Galatians 6:7, 8). It is a fact: Whatever we sow, that is what we will reap. He encourages us in this passage to continue doing good because we will reap the same in "due time."

The Principle of Sowing and Reaping is an immutable law of God's creation, true in both nature and in human behavior. This is an important concept in understanding the necessity of controlling our fences. Remember: *The Principle of Sowing and Reaping.*

Our Individual Responsibilities

Now that the two principles have been identified, let's look at the first principle of individual responsibility and its relationship to fences. The concept of individual responsibility means that my fences are my responsibility: setting appropriate ones, maintaining them, knowing when they are violated, restoring them when they are crossed, and taking care of whatever is within the fences. But before we can restore them, we have to know what appropriate fences should be in place around our emotional life. Although there are various fences for which each of us is responsible, we want to center the discussion on two that tend to create issues for people like Kailey.

Choices

The first responsibility belonging to each individual is one that should be ingrained in each person early in life. Each individual is responsible for the choices he makes. If this concept was not taught to you as a child, then please save yourself much heartache and learn it now before you age another minute.

Let's repeat: Each individual is responsible for the choices he makes. He can choose where he goes (to church or to follow a friend to a questionable place) and how he spends time (more work or time with his family). He also can choose to stay estranged from a family member or to reconcile, to overspend or to budget, to make inappropriate flirtatious overtures or to conduct himself with respect and purity.

In chapter four we discussed the concept of choices. In this chapter, however, let's look at the relationship of choices and the principle of individual responsibility. We will also look at the relationship of choices and the necessity of controlling our fences.

Making choices is not an issue for Kailey and others like her. They have no trouble choosing what to eat or wear, or where to go on vacation. The troubling issue in choice-making comes when an individual expects someone else to take responsibility for that individual's choices. People like Kailey are frequently expected to take responsibility for choices that were made by someone else. Let's illustrate.

Suppose a high school student chooses not to study for a test because he would rather play computer games than read the textbook chapters and put in the work to learn the material. When he receives a poor grade on the test, he may say the test was too hard or the teacher had never liked him. He is asking the teacher to take responsibility for his own choice not to study.

Suppose a woman chooses to have an affair with someone she "friends" on a social media site. When her marriage breaks up, she then may tell others that her husband "never understood" her and that her friends "would understand if they really knew him (husband)." She is asking her husband to take responsibility for her poor choice.

Suppose a college student sleeps late because she stayed up until 2:00 a.m. watching a movie and misses a test in her 8:00 a.m. class the next morning. When her roommate comes in from the same class, the student gets angry and tells "roomie" she should have made sure the student was awake before she left. The student is asking her roommate to take responsibility for the student's own choice.

Suppose a husband chooses to use physical violence to express his emotions instead of choosing to learn to communicate in appropriate verbal terms. He then blames his wife for saying something that provoked him to hit her. He is asking his wife to take responsibility for his own choice.

These individuals are responsible for their own choices. But they expect another (the one who is blamed) to step over the fence that defines the chooser's own responsibilities. They want that person to pick up the responsibility that rightfully belongs to the chooser.

The game-playing teen expects the teacher to step over the fence and take away his responsibility to study. The adulterous wife wants her husband to cross over the fence and pick up the burden of responsibility. The tardy college student tries to badger her roommate to put on her shoulders what rightfully belongs to the late sleeper. The violent husband refuses to admit that his choice belongs within his own fence. The responsibility of his choice and its natural consequences does not belong to his wife.

Fences are in place because they are an appropriate way to define what belongs to you and what belongs to another. Fences around property designate where the responsibility for maintaining your own home ends and your neighbor's responsibility begins. The same concept helps us see more clearly the emotional responsibilities that belong to us and those that belong to someone else.

Consequences

The second area of individual responsibility that is important in relation to building and maintaining fences is that of consequences for the choices we each make. Each one of us is responsible not only for our choices but also for accepting the responsibility of the consequences that come with the choices.

This concept of consequences cannot be separated from choices. Every choice we make has a consequence, either positive or negative. Not only are we responsible for making the choice in the first place, but we are responsible for the consequence of that choice. An old proverb states, "When you pick up a stick, you pick up both ends." When you make a choice (one end of the stick), you also pick up the consequences of that choice (the other end of the stick).

The idea of consequences for choices is related to the Principle of Sowing and Reaping. When we choose to work steadily (*choice*), we reap a paycheck and perhaps a promotion (*consequences*). If we choose to play (*choice*) instead of work, we reap a broken work history (*consequence*). When we choose to work toward spiritual maturity (*choice*), our life shows more spiritual maturity (*consequence*). Over time if we act harshly toward others (*choice*), we reap broken relationships (*consequence*).

Most of us generally understand this natural process. We make a choice and the choice has consequences—the Principle of Sowing and Reaping. The troubling issue comes not because we don't understand the process. The issue comes about because someone else chooses to step in (over our fences) to take responsibility for the consequences of a choice we have made. That person has interrupted the natural process by which we learn and mature and maintain our fences.

This issue is quite different from that caused by a violation of the Principle of Individual Responsibility. In that case a chooser expects someone else to step over the fence and pick up the responsibility that belongs only to the chooser. In other words, the chooser shuns individual responsibility for the choice. In a violation of the Principle of Sowing and Reaping, however, someone other than the chooser freely steps over the chooser's fence and picks up the burden without being expected to or without being asked to do so. In other words, the chooser makes a choice and another person snatches up the choice's consequence that belongs only to the chooser.

Let's look at a few examples of violation of the Principle of Sowing and Reaping. Suppose a man chooses to drink alcohol to excess. Instead of letting him suffer the consequences of his choice, his wife makes excuses to his boss for his absence from work and takes up the slack at home for his shunned duties and responsibilities.

Suppose a child spends all of her allowance the second day of the week so that when a friend asks her to the movie, she cannot go. Instead of allowing the child to forego the movie (*consequence*),

Mom steps in and gives her the money. Mom interrupts the natural consequence of a choice.

Suppose a young couple continually makes poor financial choices and finds themselves without funds at the end of the month. Instead of allowing the couple to experience the consequences of their choices in order to learn to make better ones, their parents bail them out again and again.

In each of these instances, someone has interrupted the natural process of sowing and reaping. Choices have consequences. That is an indisputable fact. When a person does not experience the consequences of his own choices, essentially he becomes a weaker individual. If the choice was poor, that individual may need to experience uncomfortable consequences for his own benefit. Experiencing some discomfort is one way a person learns and grows. Experiencing consequences and relating them to individual choices can be a maturing process. Note: *This only applies to natural consequences that result in temporary discomfort. Intervention may be necessary if a consequence could result in real harm.*

In each of the illustrations above, someone broached the natural fences that defined the responsibility belonging to the one making the choice. That person then took away the burden for the choice by taking away the natural consequence. The person taking away the consequence was not necessarily expected to do so; he just presumed to do it. In counseling, we call that kind of behavior "enabling." The person who takes away the consequences enables the chooser to continue making poor choices.

Natural Boundaries

Emotional fences are natural boundaries that protect and define us. Sometimes we expect or even ask others to step over our emotional fences and take up the responsibilities that belong only to us. At other times, someone else knocks down our fence to take up a responsibility that belongs to us so that we will not have to bear it.

Both of those actions violate the Principle of Individual Responsibility and the Principle of Sowing and Reaping. Both actions encroach upon the natural emotional fences that are in place. Individuals benefit from the fences that define their own responsibilities. When I make poor choices and suffer the consequences of the choices, I can learn to make better choices, an important step in maturing. Those who do not allow me to take responsibility for my choices or to suffer natural consequences of my choices keep me from growing and maturing into an independent, responsible adult.

Having appropriate fences in place and maintaining them properly help us have healthier emotions than we would have without maintaining our natural fences. Establishing appropriate fences and being alert to their maintenance helps move us closer toward emotional fitness.

For Thought and Discussion

Control Your Fences with Two Responsibilities

1. With what aspect of your life do you find the most difficulty in controlling fences? What is the reason for the difficulty? What could you do differently to bring about a more positive outcome?

2. Can you think of a time when someone overran your fence to take responsibility for something you owned? What was the outcome?

3. Can you think of a time when someone expected you to step over their fence and take care of their responsibility? What was the outcome?

4. In your opinion which of the two principles mentioned in this chapter are the most difficult to understand for parents? For children?

Control Your Fences with a Third Responsibility

Chapter 6

As noted in the last chapter, emotionally fit people learn to control their fences. Understanding the two biblical principles of Individual Responsibility and Sowing and Reaping is vital to the concept of controlling emotional fences. Emotionally healthy people have firm fences in place but can choose to allow those fences to be pliable when necessary. They maintain them regularly by checking their appropriateness, and they re-erect them when someone crosses, or tries to cross, over them without permission.

Emotional fences serve two purposes. On the one hand, they clearly delineate what belongs to an individual by hedging in that person's own personal responsibilities. They also clearly define what does not belong to that person by keeping out of his domain the responsibilities of another.

The last chapter described some of the responsibilities that belong to each individual, such as choices. Each person can choose to be involved in church ministries or not, can choose sex outside of marriage or only within marriage, and can choose ungodly or spiritually-minded friends. Those choices are the responsibility of the person who makes the choice.

Each individual is responsible for his or her own choice of behaviors. I can rebel against my parents or another authority, constantly criticize my children or spouse, or I can behave in a disorganized, undisciplined way. I can flirt with a co-worker, start a destructive online relationship, or behave in friendly ways to others. The behavior I engage in as an adult is my individual responsibility.

The second area we discussed in the previous chapter concerned responsibility for consequences of our choices. If we have the responsibility to make a choice, then we must also accept the consequence(s) of that choice. We noted that for many the issue does not lie with the choice or with the consequence, but it lies with expecting or allowing another to take over the responsibility that rightfully belongs to the person making the choice.

A person's choice and the consequence of that choice clearly belong to the chooser. The choice and whatever results from the choice are that individual's responsibilities. Those responsibilities belong inside his fence.

Responsibility for Emotions

A third area belonging in each person's realm of responsibility includes *emotions*. Each individual is responsible for his own emotions. That means I am responsible for the way I feel at any given moment. If I feel angry, I am responsible for that emotion. No one else made me feel angry. If I feel lonely, that is my responsibility. I can choose to continue feeling lonely, or I can choose to become involved with the lives of others.

I am also responsible for my emotions of hurt, disappointment, fear, worry, sadness, or happiness. If I feel unhappy, I am responsible for that feeling. It is not someone else's responsibility to make me happy.

About this time, a reader may be saying, "You would feel unhappy, too, if you had to live in the horrible circumstances I am in." Another might say, "I surely can't be responsible for the unhappiness I feel considering the loss I've suffered." Still another might ask, "Isn't it cold to say that people who may be desperately ill or have lost their homes to fires or hurricanes are responsible for their feelings of unhappiness?"

I must agree that upon first hearing that you are responsible for your own emotions, a person might think it is a cold, compassionless statement. Before you turn me off completely, however, let's look more closely at this whole idea of individual responsibility for personal emotions.

It is absolutely true that we do not choose many circumstances of life. No one chooses to lose his home to a tornado. No wife chooses to lose all of her material goods because her husband gambled away their money. No godly father chooses for his daughter to become pregnant out of wedlock or for a son to become a drug addict and waste his brain and his life.

Many circumstances are not the result of a choice of the individual who must live with the consequences. Individuals may not choose or be responsible for their circumstances. Let's repeat that idea: You cannot always choose what happens to you and, therefore, are not responsible for the many unchosen circumstances in your life. However, the emotions with which you meet those circumstances do belong to you. Each individual is responsible for the emotions he feels about his circumstances, whether or not he chooses the circumstances.

For an example of this concept, let's look at the life of the apostle Paul. We would be hard pressed to find anyone who suffered through as many dire circumstances as Paul did. Many of the circumstances were thrust upon him. He was assaulted numerous times, certainly not something he chose. He suffered through a shipwreck, again not a personal choice. He was robbed and falsely accused, neither of which he chose. Yet he noted, "We are afflicted in every way, but not crushed; perplexed, but not driven to despair; persecuted, but not forsaken; struck down, but not destroyed..." (2 Corinthians 4:8, 9). His view about his situation was that his affliction was a "light momentary" one (v 17).

Which one of us can boast of being beaten five times with 39 lashes or three times with rods? Have you ever experienced others throwing large rocks at you in an attempt to kill you? Can anyone else say they have been shipwrecked three times or in danger from rivers and robbers, from the sea, from false brothers, or from his own people? How many of us have experienced intense hunger, thirst, or sleeplessness in cold and exposure? Paul lived through all of these experiences (2 Corinthians 11:24-28).

Paul's afflictions were far more than any ordinary person would ever expect to experience in one lifetime. Those circumstances were not chosen by him. All he did was preach the gospel. He did not choose the intense reactions of others who heard the gospel. Yet, he declared, "I will boast all the more *gladly* of my weaknesses, so that the power of Christ may rest upon me. For the sake of Christ, then, *I am content* with weaknesses, insults, hardships, persecutions, and calamities" (2 Corinthians 12:9, 10). Paul chose the emotions with which to meet circumstances he did not choose. He was going to be glad because he could show the power of Christ. He was going to choose contentment for Christ's sake.

Like Paul, we may not be responsible for circumstances in our lives, but we are responsible for the emotions we have about those circumstances. I own my emotions, and you own yours. My emotions are my responsibility. Your emotions belong within your own fence.

Problem with Principle of Personal Responsibility

When my grandchildren were younger, one of the first things they did in visiting our house was to pull off their shoes and socks and run around the house barefoot. Being shoeless did not usually cause a problem unless we had to go out of the house to run an errand. We were then delayed while socks and shoes were located and put on.

On one of their visits we were in a hurry to get to the library before it closed. My grandson who was then about five or six years old could not find his socks and shoes. H e asked, "Nana, where are my shoes?" I replied, "I don't know. Where did you take them off?"

If he hadn't been so serious, I probably would have laughed at his next responses. He said, "They were by the door, but where did you put them?" I replied, "I didn't put your shoes anywhere. They are probably in the place where you took them off."

"No, Nana," he said, "I took them off by the door, but you must have moved them because they aren't there. Now tell me where they are."

Hiding a smile, I reflected on the lesson in personal responsibility that his mother had been working to teach him. She usually asked him three questions, "Who do the shoes belong to?" "Who wore them here today?" "Who took them off?" After each question, he confessed that he was the one who owned the shoes, who wore the shoes, and who took off the shoes. Then the usual fourth question came. "Then whose responsibility do you think it is to keep up with the shoes?"

He was and is a smart boy, so he could see the logical conclusion. If he owned the shoes, wore them, and took them off, then the responsibility for finding them was his. On that day at my house, when I hesitated to answer, and was about to ask the first question, he said, "I know, I know. They're my re-spon-si-bi-li-ty. I'll find them."

Daniel was young and still learning about responsibility, but many adults act in the same manner. They expect others to take care of their personal circumstances, choices, and emotions. They want someone else to relieve them of their own responsibilities. Many do not come to the same conclusion that Daniel did, "They're my responsibility."

How the Concept Works

Let's see how this concept works. Suppose a wife pouts for two days and gives her husband the silent treatment after he snaps at her. Although her husband may need to be confronted about his rude behavior and take responsibility for it, he does not make her pout and become silent. Those emotions are her responsibility. She can choose what to do about the emotions.

Suppose an employee expects a co-worker to clean up after him in the kitchen at work or do the bulk of a report that is due. The co-worker is resentful and angry, but the employee does not make her angry or resentful. Those emotions are the responsibility of the co-worker. She can choose what to do about them.

This same idea of sloughing off responsibility for our own emotions can be seen in the lives of many who have moved away from God. In my younger years, I was saddened by the death of a friend who was killed in a car accident. My friend's mother was naturally heartbroken by the tragedy, which remained an unexplained accident in which two cars collided on a lonely road and both drivers died.

A longtime Christian, the mother had provided excellent training for her daughter in spiritual matters. I felt comforted by the fact that the mother would find solace during the next trying months and years through her relationship with God and her church family. Surprisingly, that is not what happened.

She quit attending meetings with her church family and became increasingly bitter and angry. Since there was no living person to blame, the mother began to displace her anger about the accident and blame God for it. I'm unsure of her reasoning, but it may have been along these lines: "How could a loving God let this happen? My daughter was a good girl. The loss of my daughter is His fault. He doesn't deserve my love and concern."

The mother never took responsibility for her own anger and bitterness but allowed the emotions to destroy the one relationship that could give her perspective about the tragedy and comfort in her grief. Her subsequent behavior indicated that she felt justified in feeling angry and bitter because someone else "made" her feel that way. In her thinking, that someone who "made" her angry and bitter was God.

When I expect another to take responsibility for my emotions and my behaviors, I am shirking my own personal responsibility. Statements like the following indicate that I expect someone else to be responsible for my own choices, emotions, and behaviors: "Look what you made me do!" "He makes me so angry!" "I wouldn't act this way if you didn't say things like that!" "I wouldn't have done that if you hadn't (fill in the blank with any number of behaviors)."

All of the remarks above indicate a childish view that I am not responsible for my own behavior or for my own emotions. But a valid mark of adulthood is being able to assume adult responsibilities. One of those responsibilities is the ability to admit ownership of personal choices, behaviors, and emotions. As my grandson did, I have to answer "Mine" or "I do" when asked: "Whose emotions/behaviors are these?" "Who wears (exhibits) them?" "Who puts them on and takes them off?" They are mine. I own them.

If I want to have better relationships and be more emotionally fit, I need to keep my fences firm around the responsibility of owning my emotions. They do not belong to another. I cannot expect someone else to take responsibility for a choice, a behavior, or an emotion that is so obviously mine. Assuming ownership for my own emotions leads me toward better emotional fitness.

For Thought and Discussion

Control Your Fences with
a Third Responsibility

1. Contrast the emotional responses to difficult circumstances that you have observed in others. What do you think determined their responses?

2. Tell about a time when you wanted (expected?) someone else to take responsibility for your emotions. What kinds of words were exchanged during that incident? How did those words indicate that you believed you were not responsible for your emotions?

3. Think of an incident in which someone blamed God for the difficulties caused by circumstances they could not control. What was the result that you observed?

4. How would you phrase a response to a person in question 3 that conveys empathy and compassion and, at the same time, conviction that their intense emotions cannot be blamed on God?

Control Your Anger for Your Own Good

Chapter 7

I had found progress difficult through three sessions with Cameron and his live-in girlfriend, Joyce. We would move forward one step and fall back two. The major barrier to success happened at each session when Cameron, a burly carpenter, would erupt in a short-lived but forceful bout of anger. Joyce would clam up, and once even burst into tears. I would then repeat our agreed-upon guideline of not attacking each other verbally, and we would spend the rest of the session trying to recapture the tone and progress we had made before the eruption. It soon became hopeless. We were losing ground.

Cameron's anger always caught us off guard. I noticed that it happened whenever Joyce would indicate, even gently, that he might in some way be contributing to some of their difficulties. No matter how she couched it ("could possibly," "might be," "I don't think this is the only reason," "I am certainly not without fault," etc.) Cameron came out of the chute with his horns down and bucking off any responsibility.

Even though Joyce was reluctant to state it plainly, I strongly suspected that Cameron's anger was the real reason they were in my office. I soon asked to meet with each alone, with Joyce first. She assured me that Cameron was not physically violent toward her nor did she fear for her safety, but she did paint a picture of a man whose anger was out of control. I then met with Cameron.

He and I had developed a good relationship through the earlier sessions, and this one began well. Cameron discussed his view of the issues in their relationship, all related to what Joyce was or was not doing. However, when I called attention to his previous outbursts and asked how he thought that kind *of anger might contribute to the issues, he became noticeably more agitated.*

Even after describing my observations of the impact the anger had on Joyce during those outbursts, he was not willing to acknowledge any responsibility. When I boldly noted that progress in counseling might hinge on his gaining control of anger, he bolted for the door, shouting, "I'm not taking this!" He then flew through the reception area, jerking his thumb toward the door for his startled girlfriend who quickly scrambled after him.

Cameron never came back for counseling, and I suspect never learned to manage his anger. Joyce chose to continue counseling to learn how to handle her own reactions as she lived with a loved one's out-of-control and potentially destructive anger.

The Emotion of Anger

Many of us think we know a great deal about anger since we have observed our own and others' anger throughout our lives. Test your own knowledge about the emotion of anger by answering the following true/false questions:

1. *Getting angry is sinful.*
2. *Anger is sometimes good.*
3. *It is human nature to want to respond to anger with aggressive behavior.*
4. *Angry outbursts are a good way to release tension.*
5. *Unloading all your anger is healthy and decreases aggression*
6. *Deep breathing can help to calm angry feelings.*
7. *Counting to 10 can help to calm angry emotions.*
8. *Replacing angry thoughts with rational ones can help defuse anger.*
9. *Those who come from disruptive, chaotic households may be more easily angered.*
10. *Ignoring anger is healthier than expressing it.*

How do you think you did? If you answered *True* to numbers 2, 3, 6, 7, 8, and 9 and *False* to 1, 4, 5, and 10, you already know a lot about anger including a few methods to help manage it.

Exploring the Answers

Question 1 Anger is one of the most frequently mentioned emotions in the Bible. Scriptures picture the anger of Cain (Genesis 4:1-10), Saul (1 Samuel 18:6-11), Samuel (1 Samuel 15:10), David (1 Samuel 25), the Jews (Acts 7:54), and the older brother of the prodigal son (Luke 15:25-32), among numerous others. Additionally, various Scriptures detail the anger of God toward his creation when they turned away from His love and protection and gave their devotion to useless idols.

The Bible is replete with references to anger because it is one of the most powerful of the emotions God has built in to each person. All human emotions serve their purposes and are God-created. Just as hurt, sadness, joy, disappointment, and love are not sinful, neither is anger.

Anger only becomes sinful when a person chooses to display it in a destructive, sinful way. Cain's anger led to the murder of his brother, Saul's anger and jealousy resulted in attempts to kill David, the Jews' rage led to the stoning death of Stephen, and the older brother of the prodigal son pouted, puffed up with pride about his own "exemplary" behavior. He separated himself from his brother and rebuked his own father for forgiving and welcoming the younger son.

On the other hand, the Scriptures listed above show that Samuel's anger toward Saul resulted in an all-night prayer session by Samuel for Saul. God's anger toward man led to the appropriate discipline necessary for His people to be cared for and protected. Having the emotion of anger is not sinful as long as it is not expressed in a sinful manner. In fact, appropriate anger can be used to bring about good. Note comments under question 2.

Question 2 Anger sometimes can be good. In May 1980 Candace Lightner's 13-year-old daughter was walking to a nearby church carnival when a drunken driver hit and killed her. Candace soon discovered that when the driver killed her daughter, he was out on bail from another drunken hit and run and had accumulated 5 drunk driving offenses in 4 years but had served no more than 48 hours of jail time. When the policemen investigating her daughter's death told her that the man responsible would probably not serve jail time, Candace was furious. She stated later, "I felt enraged and helpless."[1]

Propelled by her anger, Candace determined to do what she could to prevent other deaths by drunken drivers. A few days after her daughter's death, she formed the organization MADD, Mothers Against Drunk Drivers.

Fueled by the anger of Lightner and that of other victims' family members, MADD worked on making changes. By the end of 1983, 129 new anti-drunk driving laws had been passed. The next year, Congress passed the Federal 21 Minimum Drinking Age Law and by 1988 all states had also passed their own laws restricting the minimum drinking age to 21 years. In 1994, alcohol-related deaths dropped to a 30-year low. Today, the justice system no longer turns a blind eye to drunken driving offenses, and the public no longer thinks driving while drunk is acceptable. [2]

Others have also been fueled by their anger to bring about change. During the middle of the last century, Martin Luther King Jr. became angry about the segregation and abuse of his fellow African-Americans. He set about to channel his anger and that of the oppressed in non-violent ways. His anger, focused in a positive way, helped to bring about much-needed civil rights changes.

Until Jesus got angry and overturned their tables, moneychangers were conducting commercial business in the temple, a place dedicated to worship of Holy God. Jesus reminded them that the Scriptures noted God's house would be called the house of prayer but they had made it a house of merchandise (Matthew 21:12, 13; Mark 11:15-17; Luke 19:45, 46; John 2:16). He used His anger to cleanse the place of worship and keep it dedicated to the adoration of His Father.

Anger can be a powerful force when it is used in constructive ways. It sometimes provides the motivation to right wrongs and wake up others to dire situations and on-going abuses. Bede Jarrett noted, "The world needs anger. The world often continues to allow evil because it isn't angry enough."

Questions 3, 4 and 5 Angry outbursts are *not* a good way to release tension, nor is it healthy to unload all your anger. The one who bursts out in anger may feel a release, but the recipient of that anger often feels as if acid has washed over his soul. Temper tantrums rarely solve problems. In fact, tantrums usually do just the opposite. Instead of resolving problems, uncontrolled anger often brings on other problems. In Willard Harley's book, *Love Busters,* angry outbursts capture the number one spot among the top five behaviors that are detrimental to a relationship.

When a person is on the receiving end of someone else's uncontrolled anger, human nature usually responds. Recipients of anger tend to respond aggressively. That's the way we are wired. Human nature dictates a defensive response to a perceived attack. You attack me with words, and my humanness wants to defend with a counterattack.

God notes, through Solomon, that "an angry man stirs up dissension..." (Proverbs 29:22). When someone attacks us physically or verbally, the natural response is to defend. If you call me names, I want to respond with calling you names. If you attack my character, I get angry and want to attack you in turn.

Angry outbursts do not usually resolve issues. They most often prompt anger from others. In fact, the original issue is often forgotten, and division and disunity result. Thus, the angry person now has additional issues to contend with as well as the original ones. No wonder God indicates that "a man of quick temper acts foolishly..." (Proverbs 14:17).

Bursting forth in anger also has another danger, one that is much more serious. God notes, "...a hot-tempered one commits many sins" (Proverbs 29:22). He warns, "Make no friendship with an angry man; and with a furious man do not go; lest you learn his ways, and get a snare to your soul" (Proverbs 22:24, 25).

Uncontrolled anger has the potential of putting souls of both the angry person and the hearer in danger. Each may be tempted to use ungodly ways to settle their dispute. All of us can think of numerous examples of those who have sinned in anger, either in what or how they express the emotion or in retaliation for another's anger. In the New Testament, Paul plainly says, "In your anger, do not sin" (Ephesians 4:26). He strongly implies that we can feel angry, but we should not sin while feeling so.

Questions 6, 7, and 8 Both deep breathing and counting to 10 are healthy ways to calm ourselves from anger. Our bodies respond to anger in several ways: blood pressure rises, the digestive system usually shuts down, muscles tense up, and heart rate increases.

In dealing with uncontrolled anger, I have frequently asked clients and their spouses to tell me how they know when they are becoming angry. They have a variety of answers, from "His brow gets wrinkled," to "My ears begin to burn," to "Her neck gets red." How does your body respond when you are angry? If you are not sure, ask your spouse, your child, or someone else who is close to you. They will always know.

Because we respond physiologically to anger, it is helpful to do something early on to calm ourselves physically. Therefore, counting to 10 or sometimes to 20 or even to 100 if necessary, may buy time to get anger under control. Deep breathing helps to provide more oxygen to the blood stream, thus slowing the heart rate and relaxing the muscles. Counting and deep breathing are both good methods to help us control our physiological responses to anger.

Another healthy way to respond to anger is with thought replacement. Anger is usually irrational. It is an emotion and not prone to reason. Anger *feels*, "She's always cutting me down. I'm going to let her have it!" Reason *thinks*, "That was a harmless statement and she probably meant nothing at all. I will give her the benefit of a doubt." Anger *feels*, "There he goes being dominant again. I'm not going to take this any more." Reason *thinks*, "His dominance bothers me, but I will not respond aggressively. He probably does not even know how he sounds. I will answer calmly but assertively."

Willfully replacing angry thoughts with rational ones can help us defuse our own or another's anger. The next time you feel angry, deliberately stop and think rationally about what has happened. Replacing irrational thoughts with reason can be a good way to keep ourselves from losing control of our anger. We will discuss this and other healthy ways of keeping anger under control in the next chapter.

Question 9: The answer to question 9 is *true*. The key word in that question is the word *may*. Children reared in a chaotic, disruptive household *may* become angry adults. Being reared in such a household does not automatically program a child toward anger. However, parents and other significant family members generally provide the earliest models for their children. If those parents show few skills in managing and communicating emotions appropriately, they may produce children who are easily angered. The emotional needs of those children have not been tended nor nurtured. Such children frequently do not learn to identify and express their emotions in healthy ways.

Question 10 states falsely that ignoring anger is healthier than expressing it. Some people *choose* to overlook their resentment at minor offenses that have little impact, or they *choose* not to express their anger at a particular time because of certain circumstances. The key word in both of these responses is *choose*. The person *chooses* to ignore anger either because the offense is minor and not worth a major response, or the time is inappropriate for an expression of anger. Perhaps the offense occurs in a public venue, or the age or health of the offender makes problem solving difficult, or their own fragile physical health consumes so much energy that expressing anger needs to wait.

The response of choosing to ignore anger, even for a specific time period, can be healthy, but *denying deserved anger and consistently stuffing it down is not healthy.* In many well-documented studies, anger has been shown to be a factor for some headaches, high blood pressure, digestive problems, strokes, anxiety, depression, heart problems, and numerous other illnesses. Obviously, the kind of anger that harms physically is unmanaged anger.

Unmanaged anger may be unresolved anger, as in cases where an offense has been committed and the parties have not discussed and resolved the issue. But often it is repressed anger. In such cases, the suffering one may spend years quietly putting up with offenses or abuse. He may stuff down the anger over a long period of time. Anger, however, is such an active emotion that it usually will not stay put. Somehow, it seems to bubble to the top over time.

For example, a wife who has been continually degraded and verbally abused by her husband may develop numerous illnesses, ranging from headaches to digestive problems. A child whose parent is harsh and angry is not able to express her emotions appropriately out of fear of being a target of the anger. Such a child may be absent from school more often than her peers are with unspecified physical ailments. Mysterious fevers and various aches and pains can often be seen in those who live under such stress. Suppressed anger may not be spoken aloud, but its voice is often heard through physical illnesses.

The quote at the beginning of this chapter reminds us that the word *anger* is only one letter removed from the word *danger.* Anytime we get angry, we may be only a short distance away from a danger zone. A small step in the wrong direction can easily lead us to lose control of our anger. When we do, we can harm ourselves and others.

We have seen that uncontrolled anger can put our physical well-being in jeopardy. It can harm those who hold it, but it can also hurt those on the receiving end of the anger. Uncontrolled anger is seen not only in those who repress their anger but also in those who over-express their anger, often in loud, profane, and soul-searing assaults. John H. Sklare, Ed.D, notes, "Just as ink tattoos leave an indelible mark on one's skin, emotional tattoos leave indelible marks on one's spirit." He explains, "Those who deliver brutal verbal or physical assaults on others create emotional tattoos that leave life-long impressions."[3]

Details of murders at many of the educational institutions in recent years give pictures of young people who let anger control them. In most cases, reports indicate that anger was the result of perceived injustices over a period of time, but the anger was not vented appropriately nor resolved. The shooters did not pinpoint their perceived abusers or may not have even known the recipients of their anger. Even if they had, the destructive, violent way they chose to express their anger would not have been an appropriate response. Their anger was out of control.

Almost daily we read or see news accounts of a spouse who has killed a mate because he or she was angry. I read recently that a spouse murdered his estranged wife and daughter, along with two other family members. He later killed himself. Such harm was done because he was angry, perhaps at his wife who had left him. The others killed seemed to be collateral damage. He clearly let anger take control.

Other Unhealthy Ways of Anger Expression

Not all uncontrolled anger results in verbal or physical assaults or even in physical illness. Uncontrolled anger often shows itself in other, more subtle, but still unhealthy ways. Rather than harming another physically, uncontrolled anger can also harm emotionally.

Criticism

A person who is overly critical may be angry, whether at the person he is criticizing, at himself, or at someone else. If you are on the receiving end of such criticism, your self-image can take a beating. You may begin to believe that you can't do anything right. You certainly may begin to think that you won't ever be able to please the criticizer, and that thought may be correct. You will not be able to please because pleasing the criticizer is not the issue, anyway. The criticizer's anger over some unresolved problem is the real issue.

Sarcasm

Someone who resorts to sarcasm can also be dealing with uncontrolled anger. The oddity about this kind of situation is that those who are sarcastic usually do not equate sarcasm with anger. If asked about their anger, they generally are surprised. "I'm not angry," they quickly assure the questioner. Yet repeated sarcasm can be a form of unresolved or repressed anger and is a harmful method of discharging it.

Sarcastic remarks often feel like spears to their receivers. Just as sharp-pointed barbs hurt physically, sarcasm hurts emotionally.

Many years ago, I had the opportunity to hear a man in a position of leadership periodically provide introductions for various speakers. I began to notice after a time that each introduction contained at least one sarcastic comment about the speaker couched in humor. The speaker usually laughed it off and made a healthy response in return. I often wondered, however, if the speaker left there feeling uneasy without knowing the exact reason.

Those speakers had been on the receiving end of barbs intended to cut them down. The introducer may have been angry for some reason. Perhaps he was upset that he was not the speaker. Maybe he was jealous of the other's prominence. Whatever the reason, resorting to sarcasm indicated a personal issue involving unresolved anger. Such anger is out of control and unhealthy.

Passive-Aggressive Behavior

Another subtle but deadly expression of anger is known as passive-aggressive behavior. This kind of behavior is often misread by spouses, co-workers, or friends. They may think such a person doesn't care or is lazy or is simply forgetful. They often do not recognize that the person may be angry at them but has chosen not to express that anger in a healthy, honest way.

Passive-aggressive behavior can be seen in a wife whose husband asks if she will pick up a special food at the grocery in preparation for the upcoming hunting trip with his buddies. She "forgets" or stays at work too long or has to drive the children to practice. He may not realize that she actually is angry because he is going on the trip and leaving his family behind.

Passive-aggressive behavior is seen in a husband who agrees willingly to attend marriage counseling sessions with his wife but makes no attempt to complete assignments or initiate recommended changes. In actuality, he may be angry with his spouse and only wants the marriage to be over. He has chosen an unhealthy and passive way of expressing his anger.

Passive-aggressive behavior is also seen when a wife gives her husband "the silent treatment." He may have forgotten their anniversary, and she is angry with him. Rather than expressing her disappointment openly, she does not talk to him all evening. He asks, "What's wrong?" She says, "Nothing." She seethes, and he wonders.

Passive-aggressive behavior is difficult to pinpoint as anger because it can look like an expression of other types of emotions such as hurt, depression, disappointment, or sadness. Even if correctly identified as anger, however, it is sometimes difficult for the recipient to seek healthy resolution. Without a specific anger-producing occurrence to tie to the passive-aggressive behavior, the recipient is often left to wonder where the anger originated. "Did I do something," an employee may ask himself, "or is my boss mad at someone else at work, or does he just not like me?"

Rather than openly and honestly confronting situations, this behavior masks itself as something else. Such nebulous behavior is an unhealthy and cowardly expression of anger. This type of behavior is out of control by the one who is angry and can lead to fractured relationships and breakdowns in communication.

For optimal emotional health, learn to control your anger by eliminating unhealthy expressions of anger, such as ones that can be destructive to yourself or to someone else. Look for other subtle expressions you may regularly use, such as criticism, sarcasm, or passive-aggressive behavior and identify the reasons for your anger. Work to replace those unhealthy expressions with open, honest communication that can lead you toward being more emotionally fit.

For Thought and Discussion

Control Your Anger for Your Own Good

1. What is the most difficult aspect of anger for you?

2. Have you detected a pattern to your anger, i.e. what usually triggers it, how it escalates, what your behavior is during an anger episode?

3. How do you know when you are becoming angry? What happens to you physically?

4. Do you have any unresolved anger? What are the reasons that anger has not been resolved?

5. What example from your own life can you give of passive-aggressive behavior? From the life of someone else you have observed?

Anger, if not restrained, is frequently more hurtful
to us than the injury that provokes it.
–Seneca
Roman philosopher

Learn How to Control
Your Anger

Chapter 8

Do you remember the clients from the last chapter, Cameron and Joyce? At the time of our counseling sessions, Cameron chose neither to recognize nor to learn how to rein in his out-of-control anger. His girlfriend elected to continue living with him but sought help in learning how to handle her reactions during his angry outbursts.

Perhaps you are the angry person that others tiptoe around. You may even acknowledge that you have an issue with anger and wish to do something about it. On the other hand, you may be the tiptoer who lives in dread of the next eruption from your loved one. You already recognize that he or she does not control their anger, but you don't know how much longer you can take it. You also may not know what to do during their tirades.

This chapter continues our study of anger with a look at biblical principles contained in many verses related to the intense emotion of anger. We also want to consider a series of practical suggestions for you as you deal with your own anger. Those same suggestions can also help you maintain control of self as you deal with another's anger. Before considering suggestions, however, we need to see what God says about dealing with anger. Any workable suggestions need to be based on His principles.

Biblical Principles

Although the Bible does not spell out specific ways for someone to handle another person's anger or to rein in their own anger, it contains numerous principles about the emotion that can help us.

Consider the following verses from the book of Proverbs and see if you can reduce them to simple principles for anger management:

> Proverbs 15:1 *"A soft answer turns away wrath, but a harsh word stirs up anger."*

> Proverbs 15:18 *"A hot-tempered man stirs up strife, but he who is slow to anger quiets contention."*

> Proverbs 16:32 *"Whoever is slow to anger is better than the mighty, and he who rules his spirit than he who takes a city."*

> Proverbs 17:14 *"The beginning of strife is like letting out water, so quit before the quarrel breaks out."*

> Proverbs 19:11 *"Good sense makes one slow to anger, and it is his glory to overlook an offense."*

> Proverbs 20:3 *"It is an honor for a man to keep aloof from strife, but every fool will be quarreling."*

> Proverbs 29:11 *"A fool gives full vent to his spirit, but a wise man quietly holds it back."*

Principles

What principles did you derive from those verses? Are they stated somewhat like the following?

> *(a) Remaining calm and replying gently can prevent anger from escalating.*
> *(b) The person who refuses to take part in a quarrel helps to prevent it.*
> *(c) Being slow to become angry, even overlooking minor offenses, helps to quell arguments and contention.*
> *(d) Maintaining control of anger shows wisdom, but uncontrolled anger is foolish.*

In addition to these verses, several scriptures from the New Testament offer insight to anger. What principles of anger control can you glean from the following verses?

Matthew 5:22
*"I say to you that everyone who is angry with his brother
will be liable to judgment; whoever insults his brother will
be liable to the council; and whoever says, 'You fool!' will be
liable to the hell of fire."*

Colossians 3:8, 9
*"But now you must put them all away: anger, wrath,
malice, slander, and obscene talk from your mouth. Do not
lie to one another, seeing that you have put off the old self
with its practices and have put on the new self, which is being
renewed in knowledge after the image of its creator."*

Ephesians 4:26, 27
*"Be angry and do not sin; do not let the sun go down on
your anger, and give no opportunity to the devil."*

James 1:19, 20
*"...let every person be quick to hear, slow to speak,
slow to anger; for the anger of man does not produce the
righteousness of God."*

Principles
These verses echo several of the same principles found in Proverbs.
How would you state the principles contained here? Perhaps your
statements are similar to these:

*(a) Attempting to damage another by insulting his character
can be destructive to both parties.
(b) Uncontrolled anger, which is frequently associated with
malice, slander, and obscene talk, is inappropriate for a
godly person.
(c) Not resolving quickly an incident that caused anger can
be dangerous to a person's spiritual life.
(d) Developing the ability to listen, to control angry
responses, and to be slow to become angry helps a person
live more righteously.*

You may have stated the principles differently, but certainly the
concepts are the same. Let's boil them down to simple ones that are
remembered easily:

Don't 'fly off the handle.'

Refuse to get into a quarrel.

Remain calm and controlled.

Resolve issues quickly.

Learn and practice self-control.

Calmness and *self-control* are key words in both the Old and New Testament references. Scriptures about both indicate that thinking carefully before you speak is vital in preventing the escalation of anger. These concepts come through loud and clear: *Stay calm and in control if you want to handle anger well.*

Now that you know some of the principles, we will try to put them together into practical steps that can help you manage anger. Before we discuss the steps, however, there is other related information that is important to know.

A Note about Stress

If you find yourself angry most of the time, "spinning out" at the least provocation, and continually irritated at the people around you, you may be experiencing more stress than your body and mind can process easily. In that case, evaluating the stresses in your life to see which can be reduced or eliminated may be a first step toward reining in your anger.

That sounds simple, but let's face it. Not all stresses can be eliminated or reduced; some just have to be endured. For example, you may be the caregiver for an elderly family member or one who is chronically ill. That stress cannot be eliminated. Or perhaps you are going through the experience of an emotional divorce, and life will be a roller coaster for a long time. Or you may have suffered a loss of another kind, and your world is topsy-turvy. These types of stresses are simply a part of life and must be endured.

While our purpose in this chapter is not a discussion of stress, the following general suggestions, if used on a consistent basis, can be helpful in stressful situations to keep your emotions on a more even keel:

Talking over your life's stresses regularly with a trusted friend or your minister or a counselor may help you form a new perspective. Often a friend or objective party can point out aspects of your life that you cannot see because you are too deeply involved. Such people may ask simple questions, such as, "Have you ever thought about...?" or "Why are you doing...?" These types of questions can help you to re-evaluate what you are doing with your time and your life or help you create new ways to handle your burdens.

Using simple relaxation techniques regularly also may help you better handle life's stresses. Research has shown that deep breathing can help in relaxation. When a person is stressed, he frequently begins to breathe with short, shallow breaths. Taking the time to breathe deeply allows more oxygen to the body.

If you wish to try deep breathing, put your hand on your diaphragm just above your waistline. Breathe in slowly and deeply enough through your nose that your diaphragm (around the bottom of your lungs) expands and moves your hand. Hold for a slow count of five. Then through your mouth slowly release the breath completely until your diaphragm is flat. Try this with a few more deep breaths. Use this deep breathing method several times a day for maximum effect or any time you feel under stress.

You may also learn body muscle group relaxation. Sit in a chair or lie down, close your eyes, and try to relax completely by conjuring an image of a place that indicates ease and relaxation to you. It may be the beach, a cabin in the woods, a spot by a river, or any other place that you enjoy. Picture yourself in that place. Try a few deep breaths using the method above to help as you relax.

If you do not have a problem with high blood pressure, then begin with your feet and work the muscle groups in this manner: clench your toes, hold for a slow count of five and slowly release, breathe deeply and relax for a count of five; clench your calves, hold for a count of five and slowly release, breathe deeply and relax for a count of five. Use this same method of clenching, releasing, breathing, and relaxing through the muscle groups all the way up your body. The last group you will clench and release will be your facial muscles. When you finish, your entire body should feel relaxed and better able to handle the stresses of the day.

Engaging in regular physical activity is another method of helping control stress in life. A regular exercise program of walking, jogging, bicycling, Pilates, yoga, or other activities that help the body physically also help a person handle the emotional side of life. Strengthening the body helps to build stamina and increase energy, and endorphins released into the body during sustained exercise give a sense of well-being. Check with your physician about your ability to exercise and what kind of physical activity would be helpful for you.

What Can I Do to Control My Anger?

In addition to helping with the stresses in life, the three suggestions above are also good ways to begin taking control of anger. Because of the cycle and escalation of anger, however, you may need other specific steps to feel that you are on your way to maintaining control.

Modulate Your Voice Since vocal tone can set the atmosphere of a disagreement, work to modulate the tone of your voice during an anger-producing episode. Angry people frequently speak in a tone that is higher, louder, and firmer. This kind of tone can feel like an attack to the person on the receiving end. His natural instinct is to protect self by returning the attack in the same manner, which can escalate the episode.

Speaking in a softer, lower, and less firm tone can serve to defuse anger, even your own. This kind of gentler tone usually helps the other person listen to what you are saying, which can move you both toward problem solving. Remember Proverbs 15:1. A gentle answer can turn away anger. It really works.

Time Out Learning to take time outs is another tried-and-true method to help a person defuse anger and calm self. Time out may mean leaving the room or going outside for a few minutes to give time for both parties to calm down. This is a time to count to 10, 15, 100, or even 500 if needed and to think through the whole anger experience.

A word of caution here: Thinking about the experience does *not* mean telling yourself how angry you are, how justified you are in feeling intense anger, and how you are going to tell the other person what you think of her when you go back! That kind of thinking only escalates anger. Specific things to think about will be discussed a few paragraphs later.

A time out can also be used to engage in some nonaggressive physical activity if you are able to do so. Activities, such as walking moderately, bicycling around a few blocks, cleaning a room, or working in the yard, can give you time to calm down and to think clearly.

When taking a time out, tell the person with whom you are angry that you are angry and that you need to take a little time to think through the whole issue. Specify that you will return in a short while when you can discuss the issue in a calmer manner. Designate a specific amount of time, from 10 minutes to an hour for a return. Any more than an hour could give you too much time to become involved in another activity and an excuse just to forget the whole issue. Any less than ten minutes may not give you enough time to think through the problem and to calm your anger. After the designated time, return to the person and continue the discussion on a calmer note.

Change Your Thinking A third method, and one of the most important, to gain control of anger is to ***change your thinking***. For most people, this suggestion is usually the most difficult to accomplish, but changing your thinking may be exactly what is needed. Let's look at what that means.

When many people think of anger, they usually think that **A** (the statement/event that triggers anger) leads to **B** (the reaction of anger) or **A** = **B**. A trigger leads to a reaction. But that is only partially correct. A statement or occurrence usually does precede an angry reaction, but it does not necessarily *cause* the reaction. Remember, the reaction of anger is a choice.

In reality, another step is between the trigger and the reaction. The process actually goes like this: **A** (statement/event) coupled with **B** (what a person *thinks* about the statement/event) leads to **C** (emotional reaction). In other words: **A** + **B** = **C**. [1]

A person's own thinking, not the trigger, causes their reaction to the statement or occurrence. For example, my husband may say, "Honey, where is my clean shirt?" That's a pretty innocuous statement on the surface. He only asked where I hung or put away his clean shirt. However, if I think, "Why can't he keep up with his own clothes? I have too much to think about with the kids, my job and the housework, which he didn't help with, anyway! I don't really care if he has a clean shirt!" then I'm on the way to a full-blown angry reaction.

After this kind of thinking, I may explode with, "I don't know where your shirt is! Why don't you keep up with your own clothes! And clean up after yourself, why don't you!" Then the tone of our entire morning or evening at home is set. In this instance, the neutral question was not the anger producer. My *thoughts* after the question produced my anger. A + B = C. In this case, B (my own thinking) is the crucial element.

Let's look at another example. Suppose I am driving to work one morning in heavy traffic thinking about all the tasks for the day and the work waiting for me when I get home. A car in the lane to my right suddenly makes a sharp turn to the left and cuts me off in traffic. I brake quickly, throwing everything in the passenger seat to the floor.

I begin thinking, "What an idiot! He could have caused a major wreck. Who does he think he is! Some people just shouldn't be driving. I'm going to give him a piece of my mind!" I may even speed up to catch him, blowing the horn, gesturing and yelling out the window. I then arrive at work, frazzled and unready for the day.

The occurrence, while unsafe and potentially harmful, was not the reason for my anger. My own thoughts caused my angry reaction. And my reaction could have led to an even more dangerous situation. In each of these cases, my own thinking led to my angry reaction. The statement or event did not.

Those who are successful at gaining control of anger are in control of their thoughts. This follows the biblical principles found in Proverbs 15:18, 16:32, and James 1:19.

How Changing Thoughts Works

Let's see how changing thoughts works. We will use those two previous examples and change the B or thinking component.

My husband says, "Honey, where's my clean shirt?" I think, "I'm a little ticked off at him because he hasn't helped me with housework lately, and he has a habit of not keeping up with his own personal belongings. But that's something we need to talk about later. He only asked me where I put his shirt."

With that kind of thinking I can answer calmly and reasonably and confine the answer to the location of the shirt. Other issues that I am actually angry about call for a discussion at another time.

When the driver cuts me off in traffic, my thinking can be, "Wow, that was close. I need to be even more careful and watch other drivers more closely." Thinking in that manner keeps me safer on the road and helps me keep anger under control.

Thinking reasonably before I speak or react to an occurrence means that the C component (my reaction) of the formula is different. Because of my angry thoughts in the first instance, C was an explosion of anger which would probably lead to an intense argument and disruption of relationship. In the second instance, my angry thoughts led me to "road rage," which in turn could create a dangerous traffic situation. Replacing anger-producing thoughts with rational ones means my reactions more closely conform to biblical teaching.

Other rational statements that can be helpful in anger-producing situations may be similar to the following:

> *"I usually get angry when she says that, but I want to be more controlled."*
> *"Take a deep breath and remain in control. Look at this situation in other ways."*
> *"I can be in control of my anger. Although I can feel myself getting angry, I will respond differently from the way I usually do."*
> *"I am gaining more control and taking responsibility for my own anger. He is not making me angry. If I get angry, it is because I choose to do so."*
> *"Calmly and gently. That's what the verse in Proverbs says. A gentle answer instead of an angry one can help me solve problems."*
> *"I refuse to become angry because she has out-of-control anger. Her anger is her problem, and I will not let it control my behavior."*

Think of the last time you were involved in an angry episode with another person. If either of you had spoken gently, would the anger have escalated? Was the trigger something you could have overlooked? With that same episode, would taking a time out or deep breathing have been helpful in keeping your own anger under control? Would replacing your thoughts have led to a different outcome? What thoughts could you use to replace the ones you had? Take the time now and write in the blanks below several statements that you can use the next time to maintain control of your anger.

_____

_____

_____

_____

_____

_____

Betty Hamblen

Anger can be a useful emotion when needed, but anger can be harmful to both the one who holds it and to others when it is out of control. It is a powerful emotion with both constructive and destructive outcomes, depending on the control of the holder. Those who live in a perpetually angry state or who frequently lose control of their anger are not emotionally healthy. They are in danger both physically and emotionally. For better emotional health, make sure that you maintain control of your anger. Use anger wisely when necessary, but make sure you have a tight hold on the reins at all times. Your emotional health may depend on it.

For Thought and Discussion

Learn How to Control Your Anger

1. What is the most effective way you have found to gain control of your own anger?

2. What ways have you learned to handle the stresses in your life?

3. If you have a problem with anger control, here is a challenge for you: select five of the verses used in this chapter and commit them to memory. Decide to repeat them when you feel yourself becoming angry.

4. How do you usually handle another's anger if it is directed toward you?

5. What is the scariest thing for you about anger?

6. How did your original family usually handle conflict? Is it similar to the way you now handle conflict?

PART 4
CULTIVATING

Grace is free sovereign favor to the ill-deserving.
–Benjamin Warfield

Cultivate a Relationship with Twin One

Chapter 9

Lennie and Carol showed up at my office for a family appointment with their two children, Dylan, age 15 years, and Abby, age 14 years. Last week Carol had explained in hers and Lennie's initial appointment that she had become increasingly concerned that their family seemed to be at a critical juncture. They were at each other's throats constantly, sniping and critical.

This type of behavior had characterized hers and Lennie's relationship through the years, but now that the children were older and more expressive, she noted that the family atmosphere had become "poisonous." Each member downgraded the others, and they had few peaceful exchanges. Such exchanges had finally become too much for Carol. "What can we do?" she asked plaintively. Lennie also expressed being puzzled about how to make any necessary changes. They asked for an appointment for the entire family.

The family sat quietly through the introductory activities in the family session and Carol again explained why they were there. Before she finished, Dylan interrupted by stating, "Well, if you would back off some, the so-called 'atmosphere' might not be so bad. You're always harping on me no matter what I do! Like this afternoon, just because I didn't tell you about needing a new calculator for class!"

Carol immediately jumped on Dylan, "You wouldn't need a new calculator if you hadn't broken the other one! You don't ever take care of your belongings! I've never seen such an irresponsible kid in my life!"

Before I could interrupt to try to calm the situation, Lennie turned to his wife to say, "Will you leave the boy alone! He's just a kid. He's going to break things. Boys will be boys." He rolled

> *his eyes and stated, "It's not like you've never broken anything before!"*
>
> *Carol cried out, "What do you mean? What have I broken?! It's you who put the dent in the car last week, not me!"*
>
> *By this time, Dylan's foot was bouncing nervously on the floor, Abby was quietly crying in the corner, and I felt as if I wanted to join her. I knew we could not begin any work until each family member stopped attacking the others. Except for Abby, they had clearly demonstrated that no one heard what anyone else was saying, and verbal "claws" were exposed in their replies. If the family wanted to move forward, learning to talk without accusations was the first essential task. Second, they needed skills in listening to another. Perhaps we could work on both at the same time.*

Is this type of scenario familiar to you? Maybe you have heard friends like Lennie and Carol as they talk with or "at" each other. You may even live with others in such an atmosphere now. Individuals in such families have failed to cultivate an important relationship.

This relationship is part of the last of the four behaviors that are important to emotional health. In the preceding chapters, we discussed behaviors that are essential to helping you be emotionally fit. Those behaviors include *confronting, cleansing,* and *controlling.* The fourth behavior that is important to anyone who wishes to be emotionally healthy is the act of *cultivating.* It is essential to your emotional health to cultivate appropriate relationships. Those relationships are certainly from one person to another, but there is another kind of relationship that is also important. That is the subject of this chapter. The important relationship that needs to be cultivated for emotional health is a relationship, not with other people, but with two essential behaviors and attitudes that I call the twins.

Twin Behaviors

What are these essential behaviors? And why is cultivating a relationship with them important? The twin behaviors are *grace* and *gratitude*. I call grace and gratitude twin behaviors because of their close relationship. In fact, they have a symbiotic relationship to each other. That is, they are two separate entities but interdependent and mutually beneficial to each other. We will discuss this symbiosis and the subject of gratitude in the next chapter.

Why is a relationship with grace and gratitude important to emotional health? Cultivating a relationship with these twin behaviors is important because the regular practice of them helps build strong, constructive, and mutually beneficial relationships, particularly in a family. If the "twins" are not visibly apparent among family members, family life is usually disappointing and, as Carol noted, the atmosphere can feel toxic. Families that operate without grace and gratitude have a great many relationship difficulties. Often the members feel distant from each other. They also frequently feel resentment toward the other members of their family.

I first became interested in the importance of grace in families through a model in Jack and Judith Balswick's book *The Family*. According to their model the most intimate family relationships begin with an initial covenant based on unconditional love between a husband and a wife. As the family grows, that love grows to include each child and then incorporates children's love with each other. The security of that kind of love naturally leads to a development of grace, or favor given to other family members, whether or not they deserve it. Each member exhibits grace and kindness to the other because of their deep love.

The Balswicks' model is shown almost as a spiral with covenant love leading to grace which leads to empowerment which leads to intimacy which then leads to deeper covenant love. And so on it goes with deeper love leading to more grace to more empowerment and to more intimacy.[1]

This sounds good and even may be something you want for your own family. If so, there are three questions that have significance for you: (a) What is grace, (b) What does grace in a family look like? And (c) How can a family who seem at war with each other acquire it? In the rest of this chapter, we will take a deeper look at the subject of grace, particularly its source and four elements of grace that are visible in relationships.

The Source of Grace

In church circles grace is often defined as "unmerited favor." The Warfield quote preceding this chapter offers a definition of grace that I like:"free sovereign favor to the ill-deserving." Extending favor to the ill-deserving in a family allows for human mistakes, immature behavior, and the acquisition of needed skills. Grace can make a huge difference in the atmosphere and the empowerment of family members.

Everyone in a family is ill-deserving at one time or another. Parents make mistakes. They snap at each other, they forget to pay a bill, and they sometimes make the wrong decisions. Children in a family engage in childish and immature behavior. They break objects, they blurt out inconsiderate statements, and they don't manage time well. But if love and grace are abundant in a family, both parents and children can learn from mistakes and begin to learn appropriate behavior.

The Beginning Point for Learning about Grace

No respected writing about the subject of grace can begin anywhere except with Jesus, the embodiment of God's grace to man. The gospel of John notes in chapter 1:14, 16-17, "And the Word became flesh and dwelt among us, and we have seen his glory, glory as of the only Son from the Father, full of *grace* and truth… And from his fullness we have all received, *grace* upon *grace*. For the law was given through Moses; *grace* and truth came through Jesus Christ" (italics are mine). Since Jesus was full of grace, we can examine His life prior to the cross to see examples of grace extended to others.

Jesus' life on earth clearly demonstrated grace at every turn. Some of the clearest pictures are found in the accounts of two sinful women. Chapter 4 of the gospel of John recounts Jesus' interaction with a Samaritan woman who had been married five times and who was then living with someone who was not her husband. Rather than excoriate her for such choices, Jesus talked with her about God and eternal life. He demonstrated wonderful grace, not by condemnation of her sins, but by showing her the One who could forgive her sins and lead her to eternal life. His grace allowed her to see a better life.

The account of a second woman to whom He showed grace is given in John 8. This poor woman was hauled before Jesus by self-righteous scribes and Pharisees who stated she had been caught in the act of adultery. Interestingly, they did not bring the man who was with her.

They clearly wanted Jesus to condemn the woman, but their motive was to pin something on Him. Of course, He knew the intents of their hearts. Instead of a scathing condemnation of her sin, He asked that anyone who was sinless to cast the first stone at her. Of course, no one there was sinless. There was no taker. The scribes and Pharisees turned away with guilt and left the woman with Jesus. He told her that He did not condemn her and then gave a gentle but clear directive not to sin anymore. How powerful His grace must have been to her life! He saved her from certain death by stoning but also showed what she needed to do to make her life better.

Neither of these women *deserved* the favor that Jesus showed them. There seems to be no doubt that they were sinners and deserved condemnation for their sins. Jesus did not excuse those sins. They would have to live with whatever earthly consequences came from the commission of the sins, but He pointed them both toward a more godly life.

The most powerful demonstration of grace ever noted in this world, however, came from Jesus' agonizing death on the cross for mankind. Sinful man, completely undeserving of love and grace, nevertheless received it through the death of the sinless, humble, and obedient One. That earth-changing occasion is the singular reason that no discussion of grace can begin anywhere but with Jesus.

That occasion at the cross is the beginning point for grace shown in any interpersonal relationship. Jesus, who was completely undeserving of such a death, went to the cross willingly so that I could be saved. What a humbling realization!

Knowing this, how can I, full of sins and ill-deserving of His favor, condemn others who need grace and forgiveness? It would be arrogant and self-righteous of me not to extend grace for others' mistakes, missteps, immature behavior, and ignorance. I exhibit those same things daily in my own life, and I continually access God's grace by asking His forgiveness for them. Do my family members, friends, and co-workers not deserve a measure of grace from me who continues to receive it abundantly from God (Ephesians 4:32)?

So the realization that no person deserves any of God's wonderful blessings, particularly the blessings of grace and salvation, helps that person to extend grace to others. In a family grace is essential for healthy relationships.

The First Quality of Grace in Relationships

Now let's put some "skin" on this idea of grace by looking at it in relationships. Four qualities of "grace in the flesh" stand out from noting the grace in Jesus' life. The first quality is *thinking about what is best for someone else, even if it means inconvenience or work for self.* Jesus' life clearly showed that quality. He was patient and giving to the thousands who crowded Him daily. He seemed always to allow time for one more person in need. Of course, the ultimate demonstration of selflessness in doing what was best for others is His willingness to endure the cross.

What does that kind of grace look like in family relationships? In a family this quality is seen when a parent inconveniences self to teach, guide, or discipline a child. Such a parent might be late to work or miss an important meeting or give up an anticipated entertainment because of a child who has an emotional need. That child may have acted out, or made a mistake, or demonstrated immature behavior. A grace-filled parent is focused on the child's immediate need for guidance and not the parent's own pleasure or need.

Let's look at how Carol could have demonstrated grace to Dylan when he told of his need for a new calculator. Obviously from their conversation, Dylan had broken his previous calculator. We do not know if that occurred through carelessness or unconcern for the financial cost or simply through an unavoidable accident.

Carelessness and lack of concern for financial burdens are signs of immature behavior. Any child needs to learn responsibility for his belongings and appreciation for the cost of those belongings in order to function well in life. If Dylan broke his calculator because he was careless and then was unconcerned about the cost, he had a need to learn responsibility.

Rather than being angry and attacking him, Carol could demonstrate grace by listening to him first. Then she could take time from her day to help Lennie see the importance of Dylan's need. Ideally, they could work together or Lennie could lead in helping Dylan.

With or without Lennie's support, however, she could develop a plan to guide Dylan toward a better sense of financial responsibility. Then she could discipline herself to make sure he followed the plan or experienced the consequences. Developing that plan and following up would be inconvenient for Carol but would pay tremendous dividends in Dylan's life. Such grace would indicate that she is more focused on what is best for Dylan than she is on her own convenience.

Doing what is best for others means that I hold my family members accountable for their behavior even though it is inconvenient or more work for me. I may sit up hours beyond bedtime to deal with a daughter who came in past curfew, or I may confront a spouse who treats me disrespectfully.

Doing what is best for others means that I help my family members (and others, too) grow and mature in ways that are good for them even if it takes my time, my effort, and my skills. I may take the time to show a co-worker who has made an error something he needs to know to grow in his job. I might help my child learn the value of money, the importance of punctuality, or the necessary respect for authority.

Showing grace to do what is best for others means that I encourage them to use their special God-given abilities. I might take time to mentor someone on a job site or at church, or I may sit patiently through one more practice for my child, or I help one of my children research the best courses for her to take in school.

Extending grace in my family lets me practice the Golden Rule. I can "do unto others" what I want done to me when I need it. Grace in action is beautiful. It allows for growth, not only for an individual but also for relationships.

A Second Quality of Grace in Relationships

A second quality of grace is *being patient with others' weaknesses and faults*. We've already noted how Jesus was patient with the two sinful women. He was also patient with someone even closer to Him. Peter was an impulsive, bold fisherman who often spoke first and thought afterwards. Jesus patiently but firmly dealt with him as Peter grew and matured into the powerful man of God that he became (see specifically Matthew 16:21-23 and John 13:5-10).

Family members who are gracious to others in the family show patience with each other. A wife in such a family is patient with her husband because he is human, he is male, and he has peculiarities and quirks just as she does. A husband in that family understands that his wife is female (meaning she thinks and acts differently from him), she makes human mistakes, and she has her own set of quirky behaviors.

Parents who show grace realize their children are not little adults but young, immature beings who often lack judgment. Because the family members are patient with each other's weaknesses, the individuals in the family have freedom to learn skills they need to exhibit good judgment and behave in more mature ways.

A friend once told me of visiting a family for a meal. Shortly after sitting down at the table, my friend knocked over her glass, spilling water over the tablecloth and onto her lap and the floor. She was understandably embarrassed and apologetic until the youngest child in the family, a three-year-old sitting across the table, piped up with, "That's all wight. Us don't mind messes." My friend realized she was sitting with a family who demonstrated grace to each other for mistakes and immature behavior.

A Third Quality of Grace

A third quality of grace in relationships is *forgiving hurts and slights*. No relationship that extends over a period of time is perfect. Because we are human, we often say and do things that wound others that we care about. This is especially true in families where there is daily contact and a variety of personalities. Emotionally healthy people practice this kind of grace in various venues, whether it is on the job, at school, on the ball field, at church, or in the family.

Hurts and slights occur in families. Individuals in a healthy family can discuss such hurts, forgive them, and move on. Many unhealthy families do not practice this type of forgiveness. They may hold on to grudges, or remind each other of previous hurts, or continually argue about slights from the past. Such lack of grace creates an unhealthy family atmosphere.

When you choose to extend grace for hurts and slights, then you are choosing to resolve your anger quickly, forgive others, and work to solve the problem. That kind of grace means that when you speak to individuals who have hurt or slighted you, you speak out of love and concern and you do not attack their character. You speak of the problem, not how terrible that person is to say or do such a thing. You also let others know they are forgiven so you can be reconciled.

Note: Forgiveness does not mean that you permit family members to get by with intentional wounding or you sit quietly through attacks that hurt you. Remember that one of the qualities of grace is doing what is best for another at one's own inconvenience. That frequently means holding another accountable for his behavior. Each member in a family needs to be accountable to other family members. But grace and forgiveness mean that you deal with the wound honestly and swiftly. You discuss it, resolve it, forgive it, and move forward.

The Fourth Quality of Grace

The fourth quality of grace in relationships is **_allowing God to work in others' lives_**. Often in families there are issues that are persistent and cannot be easily or quickly resolved. These occur sometimes because of the personality or character of one of the family members, because of habits that develop, or perhaps because of wrong choices that an individual member makes. These are tough issues that may keep us up at night worrying about the future.

Perhaps an older child has gone astray in spite of the solid training he had in the family. Family members have confronted the behavior appropriately, they have prayed and sought help as needed, and they have expressed their love and willingness to help to their child. When they have done all they know that is appropriate, their next task is to wait for God to work in their child's life while they continue to pray. The outcome is uncertain. God does not overrule an individual's will, and there is a possibility the child will continue willfully in his behavior. Nevertheless, if the family has done everything it can do without enabling the child's behavior, then they must wait for God. And waiting is tough.

Perhaps a husband repeatedly spends too much money on material things. His wife has confronted the behavior, set up appropriate safeguards, asked for help, prayed specifically and continuously, and let the offender know of her love and prayers. She then must allow God to work in that individual's life while still working to hold her husband accountable.

I realize that these comments above raise a picture of a family sitting idly by twiddling their thumbs while the offending family member acts out in inappropriate ways. That is an incorrect picture. Families with difficulties like that need to continue to do the right things. One of those right things is moving forward in their lives with full faith in the ability of God to bring about needed changes in His own time.

Grace is displayed to the offender by letting him know the status in the family. That is, family members can show the offender their continued love, their refusal to enable the offender in continuing the offense, their constant prayer, and their faith in God's ability to change others. Such behavior demonstrates the preceding three qualities of grace that have been discussed in this chapter: doing what is best for another, being patient with another's weakness and forgiving hurts. But extending such grace also clearly communicates to the offender that the family has the solid faith needed to let go of trying to work out the offender's problem themselves and their reliance on God for the outcome.

Some families with healthy relationships can fall prey to dysfunction when a family member exhibits behaviors that put the family and that individual at risk. When individual efforts have failed to bring about needed changes, having the grace that allows God to work in the individual's life is necessary for the emotional health of the entire family. Putting a family member in God's hands is the very best that we can ever do for her or him. Communicating that fact to the individual and being able to fully comply with doing so is powerful in the life of any family.

There is a song entitled "Wonderful Grace of Jesus." We might also say that grace exhibited among family members is wonderful. A full demonstration of grace can lead to improved relationships and healthy interactions among family members. To be more emotionally fit cultivate a relationship with one of the twins named Grace.

For Thought and Discussion

Cultivate a Relationship with Twin One

1. Describe an example of grace you have observed in a family relationship?

2. Was grace regularly practiced in your family of origin? If yes, how? If no, what was the result for family members?

3. What kind of difficulty does your current family have in showing grace to each other?

4. Is there a particular family member to whom you are having difficulty extending grace? What is the basis for that difficulty?

Cultivate a Relationship with Twin Two

Chapter 10

After reviewing the intake form for my new clients, I went to the reception area to retrieve them and found the couple seated as far away from each other as possible. Brady was sitting upright in the wing chair with a magazine in his lap. His gaze darted around the room, frequently coming to rest on his wife's face. Macy was perched stiffly on the edge of the couch, one leg crossed over the other with the foot at the end of that leg twitching nervously. She was flipping rapidly through a periodical on the coffee table without reading a line. She did not look at her husband. The couple's body language and facial expressions clearly communicated that they were not at ease. I also surmised that Macy seemed angrier and more reluctant to be in the office than Brady did.

After their curt, smile-less greetings we walked to my office. Brady sat down quickly but Macy immediately scooted her chair slightly so that her shoulder was turned away from her husband. This kind of behavior is not unusual for couples who are angry and having difficulty in their marriages, but I hoped it was not a sign of her resistance to the counseling process.

After the preliminary review of pertinent items related to counseling, I asked Brady to explain why they were there. Since he had made the appointment, it seemed reasonable to assume that he was the one most interested in doing something about their difficulties, whatever they were.

He hesitated for a long time before beginning his explanation by noting that he had always loved his wife fervently. He expressed hope for their relationship and a willingness to make any changes necessary for their marriage. He then recounted numerous incidents of his own "failings" to meet his wife's needs and expectations. He ended with, "I guess I just don't know how to please her. It may be that I am not aware of what women want or it may be the way I was raised or I may be just dense. I hope you can help me know how I need to change."

In listening between the words of the incidents he recounted, I could hear a great deal of thought and concern for his wife. His retelling also indicated a sacrifice of his own needs and wants for his wife's desires. But I knew that the story was incomplete, and any premature assumptions could impede the counseling process. I was anxious to hear what Macy had to say. During Brady's explanation, she had been largely impassive except for an occasional smirk and rolling of her eyes.

Surprisingly, Macy's accounts of their difficulties did not contradict Brady's. Her perspective, however, was completely different. Through that session and the following ones, I learned a great deal about the background of the couple, their families of origin, and their expectations of marriage.

Macy was the only daughter in an affluent family. Her every wish was fulfilled by her doting father as soon as it was expressed. Throughout childhood and adolescence, Macy's behavior had been frequently irresponsible and immature. Although this type of upbringing does not necessarily predict or determine the adult life of such a child, it brought a great deal of difficulty for Macy in her relationships. She admitted during our session that she had never had many close friends. But then she met Brady in college, and they fell in love.

She entered marriage with the expectation that her life would continue in much the same vein as in her childhood and adolescence. She expected that she and her husband would be in the same roles that she and her father had been—he as the giver and she as the taker. Those roles in adolescence are not healthy or beneficial, and they certainly are not in marriage. Healthy marriages require both adults to choose responsible, mature, and interdependent behaviors. As an adult, Macy chose to continue behaving in the same childish way, expecting the love and gifts that Brady gave her without gratitude for his sacrifices. Consequently, her marriage was in trouble. But Brady also had a role in their difficulties. He had failed to hold his wife accountable, and he continued to enable her as she engaged in the same immature behaviors.

> *We worked a long time on changing their patterns of behavior. Both had a great deal of difficulty with change. Brady, a kind and gentle person, was a natural giver, and Macy needed to learn an entirely new way of relating. She had some resistance to making the needed changes. Several times she expressed her belief that there was nothing wrong with her behavior, and Brady needed to make all the changes.*
>
> *We achieved some success, but because Macy's behaviors were ingrained from earliest childhood, I knew there would probably be more difficulties ahead for them unless the couple continued to grow in healthy ways. They both needed to make deliberate choices so their emotional lives would be healthier.*
>
> *The indulgent behaviors in Macy's early family had set her up for a life filled with irresponsibility, self-centeredness, and ingratitude. Unfortunately, Macy is one of many persons who take for granted the great blessings they enjoy and who do not express gratitude for what they have. Those like Macy choose instead to focus on what they want next. Their self-focus is often so strong and demanding that others give in just to keep peace.*

Cultivating a Relationship with Gratitude

Cultivating a relationship with gratitude, the twin of grace, is important for a person's emotional health and the health of their relationships. Focusing on one's blessings can lead to contentment with personal circumstances, and liberally expressing thankfulness can lead to healthier relationships.

A few years ago two professors conducted research to determine whether a grateful outlook had a positive impact on a person's physical and psychological functioning. Specifically, the professors wanted to investigate whether there were benefits to focusing on one's blessings.

Their various studies indicated that "a state of gratefulness led to some emotional, physical, or interpersonal benefits." Some groups that focused on gratitude reported fewer physical symptoms and exercised more. Other participants demonstrated more help and more emotional support for others. The professors stated their belief that an intentional grateful outlook has the "ability to impact long-term levels of well-being."[1]

Cultivating a relationship with gratitude, the "twin" behavior of grace, is vital if a person wants to be emotionally healthy. The fact that focusing on blessings helps us physically is an added benefit. Of course, the professors' work, as well as numerous other research studies, only point out what God has always known. Being thankful is for our own good. Displaying gratitude is healthy for us in all aspects, emotionally, physically, socially, and spiritually.

The Twin Relationship

How is gratitude a twin of grace? From our discussion of grace in the previous chapter, we noted that the display of grace in relationships comes first from the realization of the grace of God to us. Because I realize that I am completely unworthy of His grace given freely to me, I can more easily extend my own grace to others for their mistakes and faults.

Closely related to the realization of God's grace is *gratitude* for it. His grace to this undeserving creature makes me fall on my knees in thankfulness for His favor.

The gratitude that I have for God's grace and Jesus' ultimate sacrifice tends to make me more alert to the ways that God continues His blessings to me on a daily basis. When I focus on those blessings, I can see that I don't deserve them. Therefore, I am much more thankful for them. Grace and gratitude are so closely related that they can't be separated. They are twins, both coming from the knowledge and realization of God's blessings to us.

References to Gratitude

Psalm 100 expresses so well the psalmist's understanding and gratitude for God Himself and for his own blessings:

> *Make a joyful noise to the Lord, all the earth!*
> *Come into his presence with singing!*
>
> *Know that the Lord, he is God!*
> *It is he who made us, and we are his;*
> *we are his people, and the sheep of his*
> *pasture.*
>
> *Enter his gates with thanksgiving,*
> *and his courts with praise!*
> *Give thanks to him; bless his name!*

Betty Hamblen

For the Lord is good;
His steadfast love endures forever,
and his faithfulness to all generations.

The New Testament contains many acknowledgments of God's blessings to man and the resultant gratitude for them. Thanksgiving is extended for God's blessings, both material and spiritual, as well as the blessing of relationships. The apostle Paul wrote often of his own gratitude for God's spiritual gift of salvation and, in several of his writings, urged his readers also to be thankful for such an "indescribable gift" (Colossians 1:11,12; 1 Corinthians 15:15; 2 Corinthians 9:15).

There are also several examples in the New Testament of gratitude for material blessings. Jesus thanked God for the loaves and fishes that were provided for the multitudes that followed Him (Matthew 14:19 and 15:36). Paul followed the example of his Master as he thanked God for the food he and the sailors ate after a terrifying storm at sea (Acts 17:35).

Gratitude for relationships is also prevalent throughout the New Testament Scriptures, particularly in Paul's writings. The apostle began all of his letters, except the Galatian letter and his second letter to the Corinthian church, with an acknowledgment of thanks for the churches to whom he was writing. Not only was he grateful for them in general but he specified his thanks for certain aspects of their lives: their faith and love, God's grace to them, their steadfastness, and their partnership with him in the gospel.

Paul also sprinkled his letters with other expressions of his gratitude. He, who had been an enemy of God, was grateful that he had been chosen to serve God (1Timothy 1: 12, 13). He was thankful for the joy he had from praying for the Thessalonians (1 Thessalonians 3:9). He even urged that thanks and prayers be offered for all people, especially for leaders (1 Timothy 2:1).

Paul's constant display of gratitude both to God and to others provides a stunning display of the connection between gratitude and contentment. In a previous chapter, we pointed out the sufferings and persecutions that Paul endured. But repeating those here may help us to remember the sheer quantity and intensity of those sufferings.

Three times he was shipwrecked, even drifting on the sea for a day and a half. Five times he was lashed with forty stripes from a whip and three times with rods. He was stoned once, and often sleepless, hungry and thirsty. His life was in peril constantly from robbers, Gentiles, his own countrymen and false brothers. Once he had to be let down over a city wall in a basket to save his life from the king of Damascus. Dangers were on every hand, in the city, in the wilderness, on the rivers, and at sea. He spoke of his lack of sleep, his hunger and thirst and exposure to both cold and heat. And yet he noted that he would rather boast of those things because they showed his weakness (2 Corinthians 11:23-33).

In spite of all of those difficult circumstances, this man who displayed his complete gratitude to God at every turn, stated unequivocally that he had learned to be content whatever his circumstances were (Philippians 4:11). Paul had received a large measure of grace, and he was deeply grateful.

Enduring gratitude for what God has done for us causes us to view our own blessings through that lens. Because of that foundational gratitude, we can extend thankfulness for all our other blessings, our material goods, our relationships, and our circumstances.

Gratitude in Relationships

Let's see how gratitude is demonstrated in relationships, particularly in families. Do you remember Macy, the wife told about in the beginning of this chapter? What would have been the difference in her marriage and in her life if she had displayed the kind of gratitude that Paul did for those he loved?

Let's suppose that one evening early on in Brady's and Macy's marriage, Brady had brought home two tickets to a sporting event featuring his favorite team. Although he knew that Janet did not like sports, he wanted to share his own excitement at the game with her, his best friend. If Macy's response had been similar to the one below, her marriage might be different today:

Macy: "I really appreciate that you thought of me to share this with (A *gratitude statement*). Especially since you know how little I like football and cold weather."

Brady: "I know, honey. I thought of that, but this is such a big game and you might like it if you go."

Macy: "Perhaps. I know how much you like the Titans, so I feel really honored that you want me to experience that with you (*A gratitude statement*). Are you sure that you don't want to give the ticket to one of your buddies?"

Brady: "Yeah, I'm sure. We'll have to be gone all day and then overnight, too, and I just didn't want you and me to be apart for a whole weekend."

Macy: "Well, I know how much it means to you, so I'll go. But you will definitely have to explain the game to me. And...you'll have to promise to go somewhere I like another time."

While Macy perhaps might never express gratitude for an occasion like this, she could appreciate her husband's intent. She could acknowledge Brady's desire to share one of his important experiences with her. She also could be honest about her feelings and her reluctance to attend. Brady would have been able to understand that, but he wasn't able to understand the tantrum that actually occurred. During Macy's out-of-control behavior, she yelled several times that he didn't "care about" what she wanted. Brady did indeed find a friend to attend the football game with him, and he never again asked Macy to attend with him.

That kind of experience repeated over time helps to erode the feeling of intimacy between a husband and wife. Those experiences frequently leave one partner feeling underappreciated and undervalued. Macy and Brady had a number of such experiences.

The daily expression of gratitude in families has an amazing ability to "oil the creaky hinges." Members in such families feel appreciated for their gifts of time, thought, and material items. They sense that they are valued, and as researchers have noted, they are happier and more supportive of each other.

We can understand how genuine expressions of thanks help relationships and are beneficial to one's life. We all want to feel loved and appreciated. We want our intentions and concerns for others to be noted. Improving relationships may require healthy doses of thankfulness, but let's look at other aspects of emotional health that can be enhanced by gratitude.

Gratitude's Impact on Other Aspects

There are two biblical passages that are troublesome to many who wish to be emotionally healthy. The first passage is found in Philippians 4:6-7, "do not be anxious about anything, but in everything by prayer and supplication with *thanksgiving* (italics mine) let your requests be made known to God. And the peace of God, which surpasses all understanding, will guard your hearts and your minds in Christ Jesus."

The passage above gives a picture of someone who is anxious and worried. That person has a problem of some sort that has him deeply concerned. The Scripture indicates that the individual does not need to be anxious about the problem. He can ask God for exactly what is needed, but with *thanksgiving*. The thanksgiving part is what stops many people short. In the midst of an anxiety-producing issue that may give you a sleepless night and a stomach tied up in knots, what in the world could you be thankful about?

The other scriptural reference is found in 1 Thessalonians 5:16-18, "Rejoice always, pray without ceasing, *give thanks in all circumstances* (italics mine); for this is the will of God in Christ Jesus for you." Wow, in all circumstances?! God really expects me to rejoice and be thankful when I am disappointed, when I have had a loss, when I am going through a tragedy? The only answer to that question is *yes*. The Scripture does not change. But how can we be thankful in those kinds of circumstances?

Being Thankful in All Circumstances

Prayer is useless unless we believe that God will hear and will do something to help. Therefore, we can always express our gratitude that, no matter the circumstances, He listens to our prayers. Just before He raised Lazarus from the dead, Jesus thanked His Father for listening (John 11:41, 42). We can also be thankful that, because we are His children, we can go to Him for help. If we are alert to His continued blessings showered on us daily, we can express our thanks to Him for what He has done for us in the past, how He has intervened or taught us or disciplined us.

We can thank Him for our faith, that deep-down belief and knowledge that He will provide a way, even in trying circumstances. We can even thank Him in advance for the answer that we know He will give (Matthew 7:7-11) for, although the answer may not be exactly what we have prayed for, it will be exactly right.

"I should be thankful even in tragedy, God?"

"Yes," He replies.

"But, God," I ask, "do You mean even if a tornado blows away my house, or my child becomes desperately ill, or I have a diagnosis of a terminal disease, or my business burns, or a hurricane hits, or even if one of my loved ones dies?" His reply is the same.

In such desperate circumstances when my heart is breaking, for what can I be thankful? I can be grateful for what is left, for what I had as long as I did, for friends and encouragers, for physical touch from people who care, for the fact that no one else was hurt, for the ability to depend on God's help, for comforting words, for learning what is important in life, for the opportunity to be used as an example of faith, and for numerous other blessings. Even during life's most difficult times, gratitude can be expressed. Those who are able to find the smallest blessings during those tragedies seem to weather them in a healthier manner.

Anxiety can overwhelm us in times of trouble. Approaching such times with a spirit of gratitude helps to ease the anxiety. Emotional fitness calls for a spirit of gratitude. Cultivate a continuing relationship with the twin attitudes and behaviors of grace and gratitude.

Being Thankful for Difficulties

Several years ago a friend sent me the following email. I would like to give credit to the originator, but thus far research has not been able to uncover the name of the author. The poem seems to be one of the ubiquitous emails that float around the web for years. The message of the poem, however, is pertinent and clearly demonstrates that gratitude can be extended even for daily irritants and difficulties.

I am thankful...
For the husband who complains when his dinner is not on time...
because he is home with me, not with someone else.

For the teenager who complains about doing dishes...
because that means she is at home and not on the streets.

For the taxes that I pay...
because it means that I am employed.

For the mess to clean after a party...
because it means that I have been surrounded by friends.

For the clothes that fit a little too snug...
because it means I have enough to eat.

For my shadow that watches me work...
because it means I am out in the sunshine.

Emotional Fitness

For a lawn that needs mowing, windows that need cleaning,
and gutters that need repair...
because it means I have a home.

For all the complaining I hear about the government...
because it means we have freedom of speech.

For the parking spot I find at the far end of the parking lot...
because it means I am capable of walking and that I have
been blessed with transportation.

For my large heating bill...
because it means I am warm.

For the lady behind me in church who sings off key...
because it means that I can hear.

For the pile of laundry and ironing...
because it means I have clothes to wear.

For weariness and aching muscles at the end of the day...
because it means I have been capable of working hard.

For the alarm that goes off in the early morning hours...
because it means that I am alive and I have somewhere to go.

And finally...for too much email...
because it means I have friends who are thinking of me.

To the author of this poem I give you thanks...
because you remind me of the numerous blessings God has given.

For Thought and Discussion

Cultivate a Relationship with Twin Two

1. Does your family regularly practice giving thanks to God for His blessings to you?

2. In the next 5 minutes, can you identify 25 things for which you are grateful? Write them in the spaces below.

_____

_____

_____

_____

   Determine that during the next week, you will thank God for all blessings that you have identified above.

3. Which five of the blessings from your list above do you consider the dearest to you? Determine that you will thank God for those five in a special way.

4. List at least seven people who have blessed your life. Next week determine to thank one person a day from your list for something specific they have done to bless your life.

Cultivate a Support System

Chapter 11

Miriam sat with bent head, weeping quietly, as we talked. With considerable pain in her voice, she said, "He's just gone. One minute he was here, and the next minute as we stood talking, he dropped to the floor and never revived. The paramedics couldn't do anything." She paused and looked up, "We had a good marriage. I was looking forward to doing things together now since the kids have all left home."

My heart ached as I imagined the emotions of this middle-aged woman who watched her husband die suddenly in front of her after 32 years of marriage. "For weeks I just sat in a chair staring at the door, expecting him to come home," she continued. After a pause, she choked out, "The house is so quiet. Deathly quiet."

Miriam had earlier related information about her life and marriage, including that she had been a stay-at-home mom since the birth of their first child, who was now 30 years old. Their second child recently had been transferred by her employer to the Northeast, and the youngest had gone to college in a distant state and remained there afterwards with his job. She now told me that her sons and daughter had left just after the funeral because of their job responsibilities. They called often but were far away and consumed with their own young adult activities.

"They have their own lives," she noted. "That's the way we raised them—to be independent and hard-working. I don't expect them to give up their lives to take care of me."

Her face drawn, she stared vacantly across the room. "I'm just so alone," she whispered. To my question about friends, she replied, "Our friends were couple friends. They're just not there now." I asked about church or community relationships. She noted, "We've been to church off and on for the last couple of years but I am not close to anyone there. And I hardly ever see our neighbors. All I have done is take care of my family!" she cried. "And now they are all gone."

As we continued to talk, Miriam related that she had had difficulty finding her "place" since the children left home even when her husband was alive. Her job skills were now outdated, and she hadn't really wanted to work at an outside job, anyway. "I loved being a wife and mother. I never really wanted to be anything else," she stated.

She recounted a life consumed with motherhood and housekeeping chores. Her personal friends consisted of those she met through the children's school activities, but she said, "I haven't seen many of them since the kids graduated high school. We just don't have anything in common anymore."

Miriam had decided to seek counseling the day she found herself at the bathroom sink about to down a handful of sleeping pills. "When I looked in the mirror," she said, "I knew that I couldn't do it. I just couldn't let my children go through that. That's when I knew I needed help."

She looked at me intently and said, "I'm going crazy with nowhere to go and no one who cares. I have to do something, but I don't know what to do!" she wailed.

As Miriam and I worked together through the next few sessions, she outlined several tasks that she would need to accomplish. As we spoke more about the lack of supportive people in her environment, she decided that one of her major tasks would be to cultivate a support system. Because of her "aloneness" and because of her near suicide attempt, this task would take priority over some of the more mundane items that were on her list.

The Importance of a Support System

The importance of a group of supportive people is not confined to women like Miriam who have recently suffered a loss by death. Numerous research studies have been conducted on the importance of an emotional support system for adolescents, the elderly, the sick, for survivors of catastrophic illnesses or disasters, for singles, for caregivers, parents, teachers, and for others under stress. Common sense also tells us that being supported by others is necessary for the very young as they grow. In other words, a system of support is vital for almost everyone.

While reviews are mixed about whether support systems providing education and emotional support can prolong life in those who are ill, numerous research studies have indicated that their quality of life can be enhanced. The *New England Journal of Medicine* reports the results of research studying the effect of support groups on women with metastatic breast cancer. The women in the research study met weekly where they received educational information as well as expressed support from the group. Throughout the year's study, women in the support groups had less depression, tension, anger, and confusion and reported less pain than other patients who did not meet with a support group.[1]

Similar studies have reported similar results. These results seem to suggest that emotional support and education offered even for a short period of time can be a positive factor for hurting and stressed individuals. In essence, being surrounded by a group of supportive individuals is a major factor in a person's emotional health.

But what kind of support is needed? Are there individual characteristics that members of a support system need to have that can improve emotional health? Those are questions we want to discuss through the rest of this chapter.

What Kind of Support Is Helpful?

The Scriptures tell us of the importance of the support of others in our lives. Biblical writers offer us a glimpse into the characteristics of individuals that can comprise the best support system. To be emotionally fit, make sure your support system is built with these characteristics in mind.

Values-Sharers

Unless your closest friends share your deepest values, they may not be able to provide the support you need. If you deeply value Christ and the church, but your support system members don't, they may not be supportive when you have a decision involving church attendance or a work activity. They may not even understand why this decision presents a dilemma to you.

If you value family, but this value is not shared by your support system, then your desire to be with family members or your concern over a family disruption may create a division between you. If you have a strong belief in biblical morals and the importance of righteousness, but this is devalued by your support system, they may not be able to encourage or build you up. The apostle Paul encourages us to "stand fast in one spirit, with one mind striving together for the faith of the gospel" (Philippians 1:27). This "oneness" indicates a sharing of values based on the gospel.

Such "oneness" of spirit is the first thing to look for as you cultivate the relationships needed for your support system. This does not mean that others who do not share your values cannot be helpful to you, but they may not be able to understand what matters to you the most. Look for values-sharers as you cultivate the necessary relationships for your support system.

Hope-Providers

When you cultivate relationships, it is important that you have hope-givers. Most of us receive negative messages on a daily basis. A quick glance at headlines from your own local newspaper on most dates has news that someone from your community has committed a crime, that the outlook for the job market is dim, and that a person of prominence has died.

On the national scale, the news is even worse. Headlines for national papers note that bomb plots have been thwarted, that protestor riots have shaken a country, and that many foreign nations are having serious economic difficulties. Headlines such as these certainly do not present a hopeful world outlook.

We are generally surrounded by such negative messages on many fronts. It is difficult to be hopeful when bombarded with such negativity. Even some individuals themselves seem to be just naturally negative. When spring flowers burst into bloom and the weather warms, instead of being grateful, Negative Nellie says, "I hate spring. My allergies act up, and the garden needs tilling. Weeding is so hard on my knees (yada, yada, yada)." Or fall comes with its glorious colors, and Naysaying Nancy complains, "The hay fever has started already. Leaves will need raking soon, and this just reminds me that winter is around the corner, and I hate winter (yak, yak, yak)." You know the type. You, feeling happy and exuberant, talk with such a person and pretty soon you are as gloomy as they are.

I once heard of a church-going lady that was widely known to be negative about almost any subject. Members had learned not to ask her how she was feeling because she would tell them in excruciating detail about every ache and pain she had. A new preacher arrived at their church and soon learned not to spend much time with the lady.

One Sunday the church had an especially large attendance. he preacher was excited as he was "shaking out" the crowd. He turned behind him to finish his conversation with a couple of attendees. As he was turning back, he automatically asked, "And how are you?" as he stuck out his hand to the next person in line to greet him. It was No-No Noreen.

He thought, "Oh, my. Now I've done it. I'll be here for 30 minutes while she tells me about every twinge she feels. I'll miss greeting everybody else!" but he was a trouper, so he smiled politely and waited for her answer. To his surprise, she said, "I feel great!" Startled, he asked in astonishment, "You do?!"

She said, "Yes, but I always feel the worst when I feel the best because I remember how bad I'm going to feel when I start feeling bad again!" A person must really work at it to be that negative!

Some people, like this lady, certainly seem to cast everything in a negative light. But Christians should be the most positive, hopeful people in the world. Knowing that you have been saved, that you have an ongoing personal relationship with the Savior, and that your eternal destination is already prepared provides glorious hope for the soul. Bringing that perspective to others is an act of genuine support.

Let's see what it means to have a hopeful outlook among members of your support system. If Lisa is newly divorced, being supportive means keeping always in mind that she can have a loving and productive life in the future, whether married or single. Bashing her former spouse and relating all the juicy, negative gossip about him is not helpful or supportive. Commiserating with her about how awful her life is now is not beneficial.

Listening with the heart while holding up hope for her will be more supportive. Encouraging her toward a more hopeful future is supportive. Helping her think about her next positive step is supportive. Being supportive means walking with her through her grief while helping her see the light ahead.

Providing hope is not the same as positive thinking. Telling Lisa not to worry or discounting her pain by telling her with a smile that things will work out is dismissing her concerns. She will think you don't care if you tell her to look on the bright side when she tries to relate how depressed she is. Providing real hope is being realistic about the crisis while having faith that God will help her through it.

Wounded people need hope in abundance. Look for a hope-provider as you cultivate your support system. The first time you have a crisis, you will be glad you did.

Encouragers

A major task for a support system is to provide encouragement. Paul admonishes church members to "encourage one another and build one another up..." (1 Thessalonians 5:11). He repeats this admonition in his first letter to the church in Thessalonica (chap 5, v 11). The same theme of being an encouragement to each other is echoed in Paul's letter to the Roman church as he states, "Love one another with brotherly affection. Outdo one another in showing honor" (chap 12, v 10). Offering encouragement is a vital role in a support system. Be sure you have an encourager as you cultivate your personal support system.

Joy-Givers

Another primary task for a support system is to provide some relief from the stresses of daily living. This is usually done by providing humor or fun. Solomon notes that "A joyful heart is good medicine" (Proverbs 17: 24). We all enjoy those who are able to find humor in the direst circumstances. And how our faces light up and our hearts feel less burdened when cheerful friends visit and help us to laugh! That is truly good medicine for our souls. Look for such a joy-giver for your own support system.

Truth-Tellers

On the other hand, we also need supportive individuals who will tell us the truth. Paul states it as "speaking the truth in love" (Ephesians 4:15). Although this verse is speaking about the truth of the gospel, the principle applies in the area of support as well. Such people provide "reality checks" for our ideas, statements, or behaviors. Those who speak a loving truth make us pay attention to the deceptions we tell ourselves. They call a halt to our negative habits. As they speak the truth, even when it hurts, they help us "grow up in every way into him." Look for such a "truth-teller" to add to your support system.

Soul-Stretchers

Friends who encourage us to meditate on "true," "honorable," "just," "pure," and "commendable" things (Philippians 4:8) help mature our souls. Such a friend may bring new perspectives, or explain the roots of biblical words or provide a historical viewpoint that makes verses clearer. That person may recommend encouraging and supportive books or share new ideas or ask questions that cause us to think or research. That person may pray with us and for us. Such a one stretches the soul and helps us to grow. Look for such a "soul-stretcher" as a member of your support system.

Heart-Listeners

How refreshing it is to be able to tell whatever is on the mind to someone who listens with her heart. James encourages us to be good listeners as he states, "let every person be quick to hear, slow to speak..." (James 1:19). A listening ear is a comfort, a rest, and a help. It is almost as if we sigh in relief when we have told the burden of the heart to a good listener.

Frequently a strange phenomenon occurs when we feel safe enough to express to a listening ear our deepest thoughts, confusions, or problems. Confusions often become clear. Thoughts and ideas seem to arrange themselves in a logical manner, and solutions to problems seemingly appear out of nowhere.

I have often noticed this occurrence during a counseling session. A client will be spilling out fears, thoughts, issues, and hopes, while I sit quietly, nodding occasionally and just murmuring listening sounds. After a period of time, the client will tell me what she or he needs to do about the fear or how the problem can be solved and then thanks me for listening. The person usually ends with, "I feel so much better now." I have offered no suggestion for a solution nor asked a probing question. That person just felt listened to as she or he worked out their own issues. If many clients had a friend who knew how to listen, they could probably save my fee!

The following lines by Dinah Craik in her 1859 novel, *A Life for a Life,* express in a beautiful way the emotions of a person who has a listening friend:

> *Oh, the comfort--the inexpressible comfort of feeling safe with a person--having neither to weigh thoughts nor measure words, but pouring them all right out, just as they*

are, chaff and grain together; certain that a faithful hand will take and sift them, keep what is worth keeping, and then with the breath of kindness blow the rest away.[2]

The ability to listen from the heart is a vital need in a supportive system. If you already have such a person, be grateful. If you do not, look for a heart-listener as you cultivate the relationships for your personal support system.

Let's stop here for a few minutes and allow you time to think about the people in your own support system: (Write names in the blanks below.)

Who is your values-sharer?

_____

Who is your hope-provider?

_____

Who is your encourager?

_____

Who is your joy-giver?

_____

Who is your truth-teller?

_____

Who is your soul-stretcher?

_____

Who is your heart-listener?

_____

Emotional Fitness

Did you name the same person for more than one question? If you did, that person is a valuable member of your support system. Could you answer each question? If you could not, perhaps it is time to look for those who can provide support in those areas that you left blank.

Build relationships that can become mutually beneficial, but build your support system carefully. Cultivating relationships with those who share the characteristics described above can be an important component in your emotional fitness.

For Thought and Discussion

Cultivate a Support System

1. Besides family members, can you identify someone from your past who has had a positive and long-lasting impact on your life? How have you shown gratitude for that person?

2. Identify someone currently in your life who is helping to improve your life in some way.

3. Is there anyone that you see on a regular basis that has a negative influence on you? How does their behavior negatively affect you?

4. Is there a family member who has a pessimistic outlook? How does that pessimism affect you?

5. What obstacles do you face in providing hope and encouragement for others?

6. What special talent do you have that can be used to help support someone else?

Cultivate a Personal Relationship with God

Chapter 12

During their initial visit to the counseling center, Darrin and Tonisha indicated that their important issue was "not being able to communicate anymore." This statement is not unusual for couples who are having difficulty, but it usually masks a deeper issue that they have not been able to talk about without intense emotional reactions.

Darrin had called for their first appointment, indicating that he was disturbed because he "seemed to be losing Tonisha." He noted that they did not do much together anymore and seemed to be going their separate ways. On their intake forms, both noted they were regular attendees at a church and marked the box indicating their level of involvement was high. During our sessions, they frequently mentioned something about their church.

As we worked together on their issues, however, I began to notice a marked difference between them. By her activities and specified goals, Tonisha appeared to be a devoted, active Christian who was involved in numerous church activities and mission efforts. She identified her life goal as wanting to reach heaven. Although she had some friends from work, her closest friends were from her church family.

On the other hand, Darrin was unable to specify a life goal or goals for his marriage. His closest friends were those he retained from high school and work. While he stated he was a regular attendee at their church, he actually described other activities he attended on Sunday. He had also noted initially a high degree of involvement but was unable to point to any specific activities or ministries in which he was involved. In fact, while he gave lip service to an active spiritual life, spiritual

> *matters did not seem to be a priority for him. Both of them noted that they had few interests in common.*
>
> *Counselors work with clients where they are and with their stated goals; therefore, unless Darrin and Tonisha specifically wished to pursue the subject of their spiritual division, I could only note it and question it as a possible underlying issue in their marriage. When I brought it up, Darrin rejected the notion. He did verbalize that they were not as close as they had been, but he did not see that their contrasting spiritual contexts made a difference.*
>
> *We worked on finding areas of commonality in their marriage. If they could accept and respect each other with their differences, their marriage could work. However, it would never be all it could be without spiritual unity. The psalmist noted centuries ago, "Unless the Lord builds the house, those who build it labor in vain" (Psalms 127:1).*

Tonisha and Darrin are representative of numerous couples who are divided spiritually. One spouse chooses to learn about God and His Word and the other shows little interest. One has a personal relationship with God and the other does not know Him well. Through the years, one matures spiritually and the other grows farther away from God unless he or she makes an effort to do otherwise. Those are difficult circumstances for any close relationship.

I suspected that Darrin had never formed a personal relationship with God. He had formed a relationship with the *idea* of religion and church and had even developed a shallow relationship with several people from his own congregation. He had neglected, however, to pursue an intense, personal, soul-changing relationship with God.

I did not discuss my personal beliefs about emotional health in sessions with Tonisha and Darrin, nor did I impose my values. It is my intense belief that no person enjoys maximum emotional health unless that person has a relationship with God. Let me rephrase that: I believe that only a personal relationship with God can provide the bedrock foundation necessary for emotional fitness. Those beliefs and values have been affirmed through the years of my practice and through my continuing walk with God and through the Scriptures.

Why Cultivate a Relationship with God?

Our earliest knowledge of humans is found in that splendorous event known as the Creation. As He formed man and woman, the Scriptures note that God fashioned them after His own image (Genesis 1:27). What does that mean to be made in the image of God? We know what it means in bodily terms. We say that a child is the "spitting image" of his father. That means that the child looks like his father. They have some of the same features. Perhaps their noses are similar, or they have the same shape and color of eyes.

Being in God's image means that I look like Him. Of course, I don't look like him bodily since God does not have a body. God is spirit, so being made in His image means that I have the spirit of God in me. I am like Him and so are you like Him. Both of us have a spirit that connects us to God, and we have the capacity to feel and exhibit God-like characteristics and emotions.

King Solomon recorded that God put eternity into man's heart (Ecclesiastes 3:11). That indicates that each individual spirit lives eternally. My body will someday die, but my spirit will live forever, and so will yours.

These things let me know that I need to pursue a relationship with my Creator. I need to know the One in whose image I am made. In fact until I get closer to that One, I don't really know who or what I am supposed to be. Because I am made in His image, I must find out who He is in order to know who I am. Cultivating a relationship with God is vital for every individual.

One of the components of emotional health is being confident in our own identity. We need to know exactly who we are, accept and assimilate that fact, and act in ways that are compatible with that identity. Knowing our spiritual identity is even more important. Our bodies (physical identity) are only temporary, but our real selves (spirits) are eternal. My emotional health depends on knowing and understanding my spiritual identity as one who is made in God's image. In fact, I think that is the basis of full emotional health.

How Do I Cultivate a Relationship with God?

For those who want to know God better in order to form a personal relationship with Him, the question may be, "Where do I start?" Man has struggled with the answer to that question through the centuries.

If you ask some religious people, they will tell you to fall on your knees, ask God to come into your heart, and He will. In other words, simply ask and you will find Him. If you ask still others, they will tell you to commune with nature, and you will find God there. In other words, the results of His creation will show you God. Others may recommend various books focused on spiritual matters and written by men. They indicate that knowing a lot of information about God will lead you to Him. Still others may point you toward attending worship at a local congregation and, over time, you may form a personal relationship with God. They believe that being around God-worshipping people will help you to know God.

All of these people may be well-intentioned, but their answers are only partially correct. It is certainly good to ask God to help you on your search for a personal relationship. But asking Him to just come into your heart is akin to asking for a miracle. I may not know one thing about Him, I may never have read one word that He wrote, and I don't even know how I'm supposed to recognize that He is in my heart. If this approach were true, I would only ask and *zap!* there He is. This method relies a great deal on feelings. It allows me to *feel that I know God*, but feelings change daily and sometimes even hourly. Feelings cannot be trusted to help me know God on a personal level.

Meditating on His creation is always good. Observing the mountains, the heavens, the forests, great rivers, mighty oceans, and the smallest creatures can have a soothing effect on a tired body and mind. Meditating on the God who could create such wonders can also bring a temporary peace to the soul. This type of meditation is good for anybody at any time, and is highly recommended. However, this method only allows you to know *some of the works of God* but not the heart of God. It is not the way to forge a relationship with Him.

Certainly reading appropriate books with spiritual themes is good. Books of that nature can help a person *know about God*, but they will not help you know God. Some books are thought-provoking and wonderfully written, but even the best book ever written by man will not lead you to the intimate knowledge of God that a personal relationship will.

If these methods are not the way to cultivate a personal relationship with God, what is the way? In the next portion of this chapter, we will discuss three methods for getting to know God on a personal level.

If Darrin had pursued a relationship with his Creator, perhaps his marriage would be different. It may be that through Tonisha's example and quiet teaching, he will learn about God and discover that God loves Him and wants to have a close, intimate relationship with his created being. Perhaps Darrin will seek that relationship and he and Tonisha will have years of contentment as they work together with God. If Darrin wants to have a relationship with God, then it is essential that he focuses on three things.

Let's suppose a guy asks his friend what he needs to do to form a relationship with a girl he likes. What is the friend likely to say? "Go talk to her. Hang around her. When you are away from her, make efforts to communicate through text, Twitter, or Facebook, or even with an old-fashioned phone call. Ask her out. Get to know her friends." In other words, if you don't communicate and pursue a relationship, it is not likely to happen.

Getting to know God on a personal basis requires the same intentional efforts. Of course, we can't communicate with Him through Twitter or physically hang around Him, but we can know Him through being with Him. Let's start from the beginning to see how that happens.

First Area of Focus

A few weeks ago one of my cousins sent me a copy of a letter she had found in a trunk belonging to her late mother. The letter was from our great-grandfather written to our great-grandmother before they were married. The two and a half page letter, written in flowery cursive, was a simple expression of the depth of his love for his fiancé and how much he wanted her to know that.

The only memories of my great-grandfather, who died when I was a young child, are of a silver-haired, bearded man, stooped by age and infirmity. That letter, however, was from a vital young man on the cusp of marriage to the beautiful girl he loved. The phrasing, the handwriting, and the expression of thoughts painted a picture of my great-grandfather as I had never seen him. He came alive to me in the strength and vitality of his youth as I read. That simple letter let me glimpse a part of my great-grandfather's heart that I could not have known in any other way.

Power of the Word

The written word is like that. Letters, diaries, and journals often let us express or read the deepest parts of hearts. Writing in such a manner requires only the person, a pen and paper, or a computer. The writer does not couch sentences according to facial expressions of the one to whom he is writing. The writer does not hear a tone of voice that makes him delete or change his paragraphs. He is free to spill it out as he feels it. That kind of spilling frequently conveys emotions that may surprise a reader.

I do *not* want to suggest that anything written by God resembles the rambling letters or journals of humans who spill their hearts through their writings. I do want to suggest, however, that the first way to know God is through His Word, the Bible. The written word from the heart of God is the beginning point for anyone who wants to seek a relationship with Him. It is the only writing we have from Him.

Many people think that the Bible is only a collection of ancient writings from a number of men. However, the Bible itself notes that "All Scripture is breathed out by God" so that the person of God may be "competent, equipped for every good work" (2 Timothy 2:16, 17).

The Scriptures themselves are the greatest proof that they are from God. The Bible was written over a 1600 year period by 40 different men, most of whom did not know each other. The 66 books cover from the time of creation to the apostle John's revelation of heaven. The Bible is at once complex and yet simple, noting numerous promises of God and detailing their fulfillment. It is coordinated with every part fitting together with every other part. Only God could have done that.

Even one deliberate reading through the entire Bible will tell a person about the history of God's interaction with man. It will also make clear God's love and patience toward his created beings, and, most importantly, it will let the reader know what he needs to do to begin the steps toward God.

But the Word does more. Psalm 119 gives a wonderful picture of what the Word of God does for someone who loves it. It gives understanding, it provides light so we know what to do in life, it keeps us from sin, it keeps our hearts pure, and it brings us happiness or blessings. God's Word is certainly powerful to be able to do all of that.

The writer of the book of Hebrews states that the Word is "living and active, sharper than any two-edged sword, piercing to the division of soul and of spirit, of joints and of marrow, and discerning the thoughts and intentions of the heart" (4:12). What power is in the Word! To be able to separate the soul and spirit and even to distinguish thoughts and intentions is more powerful than any nuclear fusion that man has ever discovered...which was created by God anyway.

The Word is the Primary Source

One of the first things I learned in graduate school was the distinction between secondary and primary sources. When I was writing papers that involved research, I had to be careful about including quoted material from an author that I found in a book by another author. That type of information was from a secondary source.

My professors were very clear on that subject. "How do you know that the second author quoted the first author correctly? How do you know that the material really exists at all?" they asked. Although they allowed secondary sources, they preferred that the information I found be from a primary source. In other words, they encouraged me to find the writing of the original author, establish the accuracy of the quotation and include the correct information in my papers. The material would then be directly from the source.

Learning about God requires that we go to the primary source. We cannot read books written by men about God and find the real God. We cannot rely on what other people say about Him. We must go to the primary source. We must go to the book that He wrote. There is only one. It is the Bible.

Second Area of Focus

Now, we come to the second area of focus, but it is the most important. In fact, it is so important that there is no way to have a personal relationship with God without it. Are you ready? Let me say this boldly and unequivocally so that there is no misunderstanding: Anyone who wants to cultivate a personal relationship with God *must know Jesus.*

I want to make sure this point is clear. There is no way to know God fully without knowing Jesus. There is no other way to Him except through Jesus. Jesus is at the center of God's heart. The only way you can understand the heart of God is through knowing Jesus. Cultivating a personal relationship with God requires that you cultivate a personal relationship with His Son.

As you read the Scriptures, one thing will become exceedingly clear: the relationship of God and Jesus. In Jesus' time on earth, He stated, "I and the Father are one" (John 10:30). They cannot be separated. Knowing one without the other is impossible. In fact, reading the Word of God is reading the story of Jesus. You will get to know Jesus as you read the Bible.

The 39 books of the Old Testament have one message: Jesus is coming. From the third chapter of Genesis to the end of the Old Testament, it is clear. A Savior is coming who will "make many to be accounted righteous" (Isaiah 53:5).

The message of the four gospels in the New Testament is simple: Jesus has come. "And the Word became flesh and dwelt among us," notes the apostle (John 1:14). The gospels detail Jesus' work and service while He was on earth. They describe Him as He heals and relieves suffering, as He tells about God, and as He dies to save others.

The theme of the other 23 books of the New Testament is hopeful: Jesus is coming again. "So Christ, having been offered once to bear the sins of many, will appear a second time, not to deal with sin but to save those who are eagerly waiting for him" (Hebrews 9:28). Included in the New Testament books are instructions about living in such a way that we will be ready when He returns: what we need to do to follow Him, how to keep our lives pure, how to improve relationships, and how to relieve both physical and emotional suffering. All of God's Word focuses on Jesus.

Jesus is the mirror image of God. Jesus noted, "Whoever believes in me, believes not in me but in him who sent me. And whoever sees me sees him who sent me" (John 12:44, 45). In fact, God and Jesus are so unified that the Hebrew writer stated Jesus is "the exact imprint of his [God's] nature" (1:3).

The Scriptures clearly note that Jesus was with God from the beginning of creation (John 1:1-3). They also denote that He resides with God now (Hebrews 8:1, 2). He will also be the One who comes to take home to heaven those who do the will of His Father (1 Thessalonians 4:16, 17).

What is crystal clear in the Scriptures is the pivotal position of Jesus as it pertains to any relationship with God. Jesus notes that He (Jesus) is the only way to Him (God). Notice the clarity of the statement found in John 14:6. In answer to a question from Thomas, Jesus stated, "I am the way, and the truth, and the life. No one comes to the Father *except through me*" (italics are mine). The disciple Philip did not seem to understand and asked Jesus to show him the Father. Read Jesus' reply in verses 8-11 of the same chapter of John.

These words indicate that there is no known way for any man to have a personal relationship with God except through His Son. This means that religions that do not put forth Jesus as God's Son are false religions. It means knowing about God without seeking His Son will not bring you closer to God. It also means that any spiritual search that does not include Jesus is futile.

The reason for these conclusions is simple. The Word of God (the only Word of His in existence) clearly notes that Jesus is the Savior, the one who reconciles man to God (a personal relationship). Check the following Scriptures for that indisputable fact: Acts 4:11, 12; 2 Corinthians 5:17-19; Galatians 4:4, 5; Titus 2:11-14. Therefore, anyone who wants a close relationship with God must go through Jesus.

Jesus as the path to knowing God is difficult for many to comprehend or believe. Some flatly reject the notion that they need a savior. But a rejection of Jesus as the pathway to God does not change the words proclaiming just that concept. Those words come directly from the only primary source for knowledge about God and His interaction with mankind.

Third Area of Focus

To cultivate a relationship with God, it is absolutely necessary to be familiar with His Word and to know Jesus. But that is not all. A cursory reading of the Scriptures will not help forge a relationship with God. A superficial understanding about Jesus will not mean you are close to God. A third focus in cultivating that personal relationship is to do more.

In order to know if the Word of God is true, you must put it to the test. That test is to do what the Word says. That test means that you must follow the teachings of Jesus. When Jesus was challenged by the Jews who were debating about whether He was a good man or an imposter, He told them to try out what He was saying. He stated, "If anyone's will is to do God's will, he will know whether the teaching is from God or whether I am speaking on my own authority" (John 7:17). Paul wrote to the Romans that "by testing you may discern what is the will of God, what is good and acceptable and perfect" (12:2).

To test the Word then is to put into practice what it says. Testing, or doing His Will, means finding what you need to do to become God's child (read the book of Acts to see what those did who first heard about the Savior). Putting into practice what the Word says means serving others (John 13:14-17). It also means keeping our lives pure (James 1:27). Testing His Will in our lives means loving, starting with God first (Matthew 22:37; Romans 12:9, 10). And it means actively telling others about Him (Matthew 28:19, 20).

When Jesus was on earth, He spent his time helping relieve the suffering of multitudes of people. He sacrificed sleep, food, and time to teach and train disciples and to give hope and help to as many as He could. As Peter succinctly put it, He "went about doing good" (Acts 10:38).

Those who practice the same kinds of things can enjoy a close familial relationship with Him (Matthew 12:50). In fact, Jesus described those people as His brother and sister and mother. What a picture that presents--the intimate circle of a family gathered around their Father. Now, that is a close personal relationship! If you want to cultivate a relationship with God, you cannot do it unless you put into practice what you find in His Will.

Putting It All Together

Let's briefly recap what we have discussed thus far about a personal relationship with God. For the first step in cultivating a relationship with God, you must read the Bible to have even a surface knowledge about Him and His interactions with man. Reading God's Word will naturally lead you to the second step, which is knowing Jesus. Then, you must work to obey His commands in order to be in Him and follow Jesus to put His Words into action in your life. You must grow into the image of Jesus.

That's it. That is the way to know God on a personal basis: (a) Learn about Him through His Word, (b) seek to know Jesus and what you have to do to have the salvation that He offers (Read the book of Acts to see what people did when they heard the gospel of Jesus), and (c) spend the rest of your life modeling your life after His. Do what the Word says. That means praying like Jesus did, living in purity of mind and heart, giving yourself in service to others, and loving God with all your soul, strength, mind, and heart. If you do those things, you will have cultivated the greatest relationship in this world. That relationship is the greatest because it is the only one that is eternal. The relationship with God is so important that I believe a person cannot enjoy maximum emotional health without it.

Summary on Emotional Health

In this book we have put forth the premise that emotional health depends on confronting issues, cleansing certain behaviors, controlling other behaviors, and cultivating specific relationships. Those actions can be dependent on a relationship with God.

If you want to know how to confront people about current issues or past offenses, God gives you an outline of how to do it. If you want to cleanse your life of deliberate sins and a wild pursuit of happiness, you cannot do it except through following God's laws. If you want to control your fences and your anger, God tells you what fences are appropriate and what you need to do to maintain them. He also gives guidance in managing your anger in constructive ways. If you want to know about cultivating relationships with grace, gratitude, and a support system, you will find the blueprints in His Word.

Although cultivating a personal relationship with God is the last chapter in this book, it is actually the step that needs to come first. You can be successful in confronting issues of difficulty, in cleansing your life of destructive behaviors, in controlling behaviors that are out of control, and in cultivating relationships with grace, gratitude, and other people. That success may bring you relative peace to your life. It may help the quality of your relationships. It might even bring you closer to emotional fitness. But success in those areas will not save your soul or take you to heaven. The only thing that will do that is a personal relationship with God and His Son (1 John 5:15-17).

Because that personal relationship is vital, it is the foundation of complete emotional health. The emotional fitness of many is connected to the quality and duration of their human relationships. When those relationships are difficult and rocky, emotional stability is harder to obtain. When their relationships bring more pain than joy, their emotions seesaw from one extreme to the other. In those cases, emotional fitness is elusive.

While human relationships may disappoint, there is one relationship that will not. Walking with God brings all humans what they want earthly relationships to bring them: true stability and security (1 John 5:13), peace (Philippians 4:7), and complete commitment (James 1:17). Be sure, for maximum emotional fitness, that you cultivate the most important relationship of all—the one that you have with God. That relationship has eternal consequences.

"Grace to you and peace from God our Father and the Lord Jesus Christ" (Romans 1:7).

For Thought and Discussion

Cultivate a Personal Relationship with God

1. Do you feel that you have a strong personal relationship with God? How do you know that you do?

2. If you answered "*No*" to question 1, what is one obstacle that has kept you from developing a relationship?

3. If you have a personal relationship with God, are you divided with other family members who do not? How does that impact your relationship with each other?

References

Introduction
[1] Henry Lodge, "You Can Stop 'Normal' Aging," *Parade*, March 18, 2007, 6-7.
[2] Dan Allendar and Tremper Longman. *The Cry of the Soul: How Our Emotions Reveal Our Deepest Questions about God.* (Colorado Springs: NavPress, 1994), 25-26.

Chapter 1
[1] James Dobson, *Love Must Be Tough.* (Waco: Word, 1983), 59.

Chapter 2
[1] Nathaniel Hawthorne, *The House of the Seven Gables.* (New York: Pocket Books, 2007), 139.
[2] Robert Enright et al, "The Psychology of Interpersonal Forgiveness," in *Exploring Forgiveness,* ed. Robert D. Enright and Joanna North. (Madison: University of Wisconsin, 1998), 47.

Chapter 3
[1] Robert Frost, *Mountain Interval.* New York: Henry Holt and Company, 1920;. Accessed August 6, 2012. http://bartleby.com/119/.
[2] Hall, Mark. *Slow Fade.* EMI Christian Music Group, 2007.

Chapter 4
[1] M. Dittman, "Hughes' Germ Phobia Revealed in Psychological Autopsy," *American Psychological Association.* July 2005, 102.
[2] Dotson Rader, "I Rose from the Ashes," *Parade*, April 20, 2008, 7-8.
[3] Nathaniel Hawthorne, *"Passages," in The American Note-Books of Nathaniel Hawthorne,* ed. Sophia Hawthorne. Boston:

Houghton, Mifflin, 1868, 1883. Accessed August 1, 2012. http://
eldred.ne.mediaone.net/nh/pfan01.html.

Chapter 7

[1]"Candy Lightner Biography," *Encyclopedia of World Biography*,
Thomson-Gale, 2005-2006. Accessed July 23, 2012. http://
bookrags.com/biography/candy_lightner/

[2]MADD, "Milestones: 25 Years of Making a Difference." Accessed
July 24, 2012. http://www.madd.org/about-us/history/
madd25thhistory.pdf.

[1]John Sklare, "Emotional Tattoos." Accessed January 30, 2012. http://
Lifescript.com/Soul/Self/Growth/Emotional_Tattoos.aspx.

Chapter 8

[1]The A+B=C idea is based upon the A-B-C theory of personality in
Albert Ellis' Rational Emotive Behavioral Theory. In that theory,
emotional issues result from an individual's belief system rather
than from a triggering event; i.e. A (actual event) +B (belief system)
leads to C (emotional consequence).

Chapter 9

[1]Jack O. Balswick and Judith K. Balswick. *The Family: A Christian
Perspective on the Contemporary Home*. Grand Rapids: Baker,
1999.

Chapter 10

[1]Robert Emmons and Michael McCullough. "Counting Blessings
Versus Burdens: An Experimental Investigation of Gratitude
and Sub jective Well-Being in Life," *Journal of Personality and
Social Psychology*. 84 (2003): 377-389.

Chapter 11

[1]Pamela Goodwin et al. "The Effect of Group Psychosocial Support
on Survival in Metastatic Breast Cancer," *New England Journal
of Medicine*. 345 (2001): 1719-1726. Accessed July 24, 2012.
doi:10.1056/011871.

[2]"Dinah Craik," *American Libraries*. Accessed July 30, 2012.
http:archive.org/stream/lifeforlife02crai#page/84/mode/2up.

About the Author

Betty Hamblen is a counselor focusing on marriage and family issues for the Alpha Center. She has been an instructor in both a secondary school and in universities and has also served as an educational consultant to the healthcare industry. Betty holds Master's degrees in English and in counseling and a Ph.D. in adult education. She is a sought-after speaker for business and civic groups, as well as for women's groups in churches. Betty and her husband, Willie, live in Florence, Alabama.